H

Moral Responsibility

Key Concepts in Philosophy

Moral Responsibility

Matthew Talbert

polity

Copyright © Matthew Talbert 2016

The right of Matthew Talbert to be identified as Author of this Work has been asserted in accordance with the UK Copyright, Designs and Patents Act 1988.

First published in 2016 by Polity Press

Polity Press
65 Bridge Street
Cambridge CB2 1UR, UK

Polity Press
350 Main Street
Malden, MA 02148, USA

ISBN-13: 978-0-7456-8058-3
ISBN-13: 978-0-7456-8059-0 (pb)

A catalogue record for this book is available from the British Library.

Library of Congress Cataloging-in-Publication Data

Talbert, Matthew.
  Moral responsibility : an introduction / Matthew Talbert.
     pages cm. – (Key concepts in philosophy)
  Includes bibliographical references and index.
  ISBN 978-0-7456-8058-3 (hardcover : alk. paper) – ISBN 0-7456-8058-5
(hardcover : alk. paper) – ISBN 978-0-7456-8059-0 (pbk. : alk. paper) – ISBN
0-7456-8059-3 (pbk. : alk. paper) 1. Responsibility. I. Title.
  BJ1451.T345 2016
  170–dc23
                                    2015016785

Typeset in 10.5 on 12 pt Sabon
by Toppan Best-set Premedia Limited
Printed and bound in the UK by CPI Group (UK) Ltd, Croydon

The publisher has used its best endeavours to ensure that the URLs for external websites referred to in this book are correct and active at the time of going to press. However, the publisher has no responsibility for the websites and can make no guarantee that a site will remain live or that the content is or will remain appropriate.

Every effort has been made to trace all copyright holders, but if any have been inadvertently overlooked the publisher will be pleased to include any necessary credits in any subsequent reprint or edition.

For further information on Polity, visit our website: politybooks.com

For Elizabeth

Contents

Acknowledgments

I'd like to thank Emma Hutchinson and Pascal Porcheron at Polity (as well as the anonymous reviewers they engaged) for their advice on my book proposal and comments on my manuscript. I'd also like to thank Caroline Richmond for her fine work copy-editing the manuscript. John Martin Fischer and Dana Nelkin were kind enough to look over portions of the manuscript, and I thank them for that. Over the years, many people have helped me to develop some of the ideas that I present here; of these official and unofficial teachers, I'd particularly like to acknowledge John Martin Fischer, Pamela Hieronymi, Dana Nelkin, David Shoemaker, Angela Smith, and Gary Watson.

Introduction

This book introduces the concept of moral responsibility (as it is used in contemporary philosophy) and explores the justifiability of the moral practices associated with holding people responsible for their behavior. Among the most important and familiar of these practices are *moral praise* and *moral blame*. Praise and blame depend on moral responsibility in the sense that people are open to these responses only if they are morally responsible for the behaviors for which they are praised or blamed. Typically, a person is open to blame only if she is morally responsible for behavior that is wrong (or bad) and she is open to praise only if she is morally responsible for behavior that is right (or good).

Interestingly, while a person isn't blameworthy or praiseworthy unless she is morally responsible, it does seem possible to be morally responsible for behavior that is neither right nor wrong and is thus neither praiseworthy nor blameworthy. This last claim may seem strange: How can someone be morally responsible for twiddling her thumbs or for ordering Pepsi instead of Coke if there's nothing morally interesting about these behaviors?

Despite the initial peculiarity, we should allow for the possibility just described because what really seems to matter for moral responsibility is not that a person's action is either right or wrong *but rather that the person is related to the action in a certain way.* We might think, for example, that a person's action needs to belong to her in a particular way, or that she needs to have exercised a certain sort of control over the action, in order to be morally responsible for it. Philosophers debate the precise nature and form of the relational requirements that apply to moral responsibility, but in general it doesn't seem that fulfillment of these requirements depends on an agent's behavior being either right or wrong. We should allow, then, that, regardless of whether an agent's behavior is good, bad, or indifferent, she can be morally responsible for that behavior as long as she bears the right relation to it.

Of course, we won't be much concerned in this book with moral responsibility for indifferent behavior. Indeed, we won't even be that much concerned with moral responsibility for praiseworthy behavior. In this book, as in most philosophical treatments of moral responsibility, our focus will tend to fall on moral responsibility for bad behavior: that is, on blameworthiness. Why do philosophers focus on moral blame? Part of the reason is that most philosophers assume that praise and blame are symmetrical and that the kind of relation that one must bear to a bad action in order to be blameworthy for it is the same kind of relation that one must bear to a good action in order to be praiseworthy for it. This assumption has been questioned (Wolf 1980, 1990; Nelkin 2011), but, if it is right, we learn something about praiseworthiness when we uncover the conditions that apply to blameworthiness. Of course, by this logic, philosophers might as well focus on praiseworthiness as on blameworthiness, and yet that's not what happens.

The deeper reason for philosophers' disproportionate interest in blame is that there is often more at stake in cases of blame than in cases of praise. To be blamed for something – to be subjected to another person's scorn and recrimination, to be avoided, ostracized, or punished – can be extremely unpleasant and even dangerous. It follows that we ought to make sure that we blame people only when they deserve it, and this means that we need to have a reasonably well-developed understanding of what makes a person blameworthy and what excuses a person from blame. On the other hand, while it may in some sense be unfair or unjust to praise a person who does not deserve praise, it is typically not unpleasant or harmful to be the target of undeserved praise.

Since we seem to have less interest in avoiding inappropriate praise than we do inappropriate blame, it's perhaps natural that philosophers have spent more time thinking about what it takes for a person to be a fair target of moral blame.

Before getting into debates about what it takes for a person to be morally responsible for her behavior, it will be helpful to consider the many different – and potentially confusing – ways that English speakers employ talk of "responsibility." I address this issue in roughly the first third of chapter 1. The rest of that chapter introduces readers to debates about the compatibility of free will and determinism. The literature on moral responsibility can't be cleanly disconnected from the literature on free will. However, since this book attempts to focus on the former topic, I try at the end of chapter 1 to distinguish the questions about moral responsibility with which I will be concerned from questions about free will. In chapter 2, I outline some general approaches to moral responsibility and introduce concepts and distinctions that will be useful for understanding the debates described in subsequent chapters; I also identify the approach to moral responsibility that I personally favor and to which I will often return in this book. In chapter 3, I turn to the question of whether a person's social context or bad luck can undermine her moral responsibility. It's here that we encounter arguments for skepticism about moral responsibility for the first time. In chapter 4, the focus is on the way that psychological impairments might (or might not) undermine moral responsibility. Finally, chapter 5 considers recent debates about how a person's awareness of the consequences and moral status of her actions can affect her moral responsibility. In this final chapter, we encounter additional grounds for skepticism about moral responsibility.

When readers finish this book, they should have a good sense of how contemporary philosophers approach the subject of moral responsibility and, indeed, will be in a position to begin to form their own conclusions about what's required – in terms of ownership and control of actions, psychological capacities, and moral knowledge – for a person to be held morally responsible for her behavior. I also hope that readers begin to see how the various debates about moral responsibility fit together. To this end, I close each chapter with concluding remarks meant to highlight its themes and to relate these themes to earlier discussions. Finally, in order to guide future reading and research, I include at the end of each chapter brief suggestions for additional reading.

1
Responsibility, Moral Responsibility, and Free Will

When philosophers talk about "moral responsibility" they usually have in mind a relationship that can hold between people and the actions they perform, or between people and the consequences of their actions. We typically say that a person is "morally responsible *for*" an action or a consequence: we say, for example, "Clyde is morally responsible for robbing the bank" or "Clyde is morally responsible for the fact that the bank was robbed." A person can also be morally responsible for *not* performing a certain action or for the consequences of failing to act in a certain way. Suppose that Clyde could have easily saved the life of a child drowning in a shallow pool but that he chose not to because he just didn't care about saving the child's life. In this case, if the child drowns, it would be natural to say that Clyde is morally responsible (and presumably blameworthy) for the child's death.

Though we'll encounter more detailed approaches in the next chapter, a good place to start is to think of an assertion such as "Clyde is morally responsible for robbing the bank" as attributing behavior to Clyde in a way that makes certain responses toward him appropriate. Since robbing banks is usually a morally bad thing to do, if Clyde is morally responsible for robbing a bank, then it is probably appropriate to make a negative moral assessment of Clyde and to blame him on account of his behavior. On the other hand, if Clyde were morally responsible for foiling a robbery or for saving a drowning child, then it would probably be appropriate to make a positive moral assessment of him and to praise him for his behavior. I say "probably," because sometimes people perform actions that would ordinarily be praiseworthy, but they do so for reasons that don't reflect well on them. Suppose, for example, that, as Bonnie was making her escape from a bank robbery, she paused to pull a drowning child from a fountain, but only because she wanted to use the child as a human shield. It would be odd to praise Bonnie for what she did even if we are glad that she did not let the child drown. In a similar way, we might revise our judgment about Clyde's blameworthiness if we learned that, when he robs banks, he takes money only from the accounts of far worse criminals and gives it all to worthy charities. Clyde would still be morally responsible for his behavior in the sense that it would still be *his* behavior, but, if his actions now seem less morally bad than they otherwise would, his actions also provide less basis for moral blame.

1.1   Varieties of Responsibility

An initial problem for attempts to characterize moral responsibility is that the words "responsible" and "responsibility" are used in several different ways in English. These usages are unified to the degree that they involve either the idea that a person is liable to give an account – a *response* – for some state of affairs or the related idea that a person is subject to certain obligations and is therefore answerable to a standard defined by those obligations: in other words, the responsible person is liable to a response from others.

H. L. A. Hart, the great twentieth-century philosopher of law, illustrates the diversity of our talk about responsibility with the following vignette about a drunken sea captain and the fate of his ship:

> As captain of the ship, X was responsible for the safety of his passengers and crew. But on the last voyage he got drunk every night and was responsible for the loss of the ship with all aboard. It was rumored that he was insane, but the doctors

considered that he was responsible for his actions. Throughout the voyage he behaved quite irresponsibly, and various incidents in his career showed that he was not a responsible person. He always maintained that the exceptional winter storms were responsible for the loss of the ship, but in the legal proceedings brought against him he was found criminally responsible for his negligent conduct, and in separate civil proceedings he was held legally responsible for the loss of life and property. He is still alive and he is morally responsible for the deaths of many women and children. (1968: 211)

Role Responsibility

Let's give Hart's captain the name "Jack." Since Jack is captain of his ship, he has an important duty with respect to its passengers and crew – he is supposed to ensure their safety. We can express this thought by saying that a captain is "responsible for" the safety of his or her passengers and crew; we could also say that their safety is a captain's "responsibility." Here the word "responsibility" picks out a specific duty or obligation that captains have. A captain has this duty – this responsibility – simply because he or she occupies the role of captain. Similarly, in virtue of being a parent, a person acquires certain duties: a child is its parent's responsibility and the parent is responsible for the child's health, welfare, upbringing, and so on.

A good captain performs the duties associated with being a captain well and a good parent performs the duties associated with being a parent well. It is common to hear such people described as a "responsible captain" or a "responsible parent." Of course, the same person might be both a responsible captain and an irresponsible parent. Here the word "responsible" commends a person's behavior relative to the standards that apply to the role that the person occupies. We also use this sense of "responsible" in a more general way: Captain Jack is not just an irresponsible captain; it's also said that he "was not a responsible person." In other words, he's generally not the sort of person that you can rely on to fulfill his obligations.

Just as role-dependent duties are sometimes called "responsibilities," we occasionally see the phrase "moral responsibility" used to refer to moral duties more generally. For example, in light of reports that retired National Football League players have an increased risk of dementia, a sportswriter recently wondered whether it is "morally responsible to enjoy this sport" (Ryan 2013). The suggestion is that, because of the injuries done to players, perhaps contributing to the NFL's profitability is a morally bad thing to do. Similarly, US Congressman Tom McClintock was recently asked in an interview for his opinion about President Barack Obama's stance on the use of military force against Syria (Goodwyn 2013). McClintock said, "The president has been very reluctant to get involved in Syria, but he says that with the use of chemical weapons, of gas, that there's a moral responsibility here. What about that issue of moral responsibility?" Again, the idea is that a "moral responsibility" is a moral obligation. Generally, this is *not* how philosophers talk about moral responsibility: the focus is not on *having* moral responsibilities (in the sense of having obligations) but, rather, on whether we *are* morally responsible for the fact that we did, or did not, live up to our obligations.

Causal Responsibility

We also talk about responsibility in the context of assigning *causal* responsibility for various events and outcomes: we say that someone or something is responsible for an event because he, she, or it caused it to occur. While Captain Jack "maintained that the exceptional winter storms were responsible for the loss of the ship," Hart's story tells us that Jack himself is "responsible for the loss of the ship with all aboard." Hart tells us, in other words, that Jack caused the wreck even though Jack would like us to believe that it was the winter storms that did it.

Causation is a complicated topic. This is illustrated by the fact that Jack's behavior and the weather might both have had genuine roles to play in explaining why the ship sank. Let's suppose that, even if there were unprecedented winter storms, the ship would not have sunk had Jack been sober and able to attend to his duties. When we have this fact in mind, it might be natural to say that Jack's behavior caused the wreck. But let us also suppose that, even given Jack's drunkenness, the ship would not have sunk if it had not encountered such bad storms – in other words, the captain's drunkenness was not by itself enough to cause the wreck. It might seem now that the storm is partly *to blame* for the wreck after all. (Of course I am using "blame" here in a purely causal, non-moral sense – even if the weather did cause the ship to sink, it's not a candidate for moral blame.) And what if the ship had been better built so as to withstand harsh weather? What if the ship had never left port or had sailed a different route? What if the first officer had relieved Jack of command? Tragedy might have been prevented in each of these cases. So what really caused the ship to sink?

Fortunately, it's not our job to decide on a single factor that caused Jack's ship to sink. All the factors mentioned above might consistently be cited in an account of the ship's fate. The factors that seem most relevant to us will depend in part on the perspective from which we approach the subject. An engineer interested in preventing future wrecks might focus on aspects of the ship's construction, while a meteorologist might be more interested in the unusual weather. Of course, the captain's role in the ship's fate is particularly interesting since he was specifically charged with the ship's safety – it was his responsibility – and Jack's repeated episodes of drunkenness were hardly compatible with attending to his duty.

We can say this much at least: in normal cases, we typically hold people morally responsible for actions and outcomes only if they played a direct or indirect causal role in bringing these things about. (Cases of omission present a difficulty here: Clyde may be morally responsible for a child's death if he lets the child drown, but, if Clyde didn't *do* anything, did he *cause* the child's death?) However, causal responsibility is not *enough* for moral responsibility because a person can cause an outcome without being morally responsible for it. Suppose that you foolishly let your two-year-old sister play with your fancy (and delicate) new phone and that she drops it on the floor, cracking its glass screen. Your sister may bear at least partial causal responsibility for the damage done to your phone, but you should not hold her morally responsible for this outcome. This means that, while you might be upset or even angry that your phone was damaged, it would not be appropriate for you to respond to your sister with the sort of moral condemnation and moral anger that characterizes blame.

One might be tempted to say, "It's not her fault," on your sister's behalf. However, in one way, this claim is false. After all, your sister is the one who dropped the phone, so it's natural to say that *she* broke it. But talk of being "at fault" does not aim solely at picking out causes. Your sister broke your phone, but doing so was not her fault in the sense that she can't be (morally) *faulted* for what she did. In other words, the fact that she broke your phone does not suggest or stem from a moral fault in her. And that's why you don't, or at least shouldn't, blame you sister for breaking the phone. Things would be very different if your seventeen-year-old brother broke your new phone on purpose because he was angry that he had to make do with an older model. With your brother, moral condemnation and moral anger might be entirely appropriate. The reason for this is that your brother's behavior has a kind of moral significance for you that your sister's behavior cannot have, and this is because, among other things, your brother knew what he was doing and he acted on purpose when he broke your phone.

Causal and moral responsibility can come apart in other ways as well. Suppose that Captain Jack did not voluntarily become drunk but that his first officer spiked his morning coffee with LSD, and it was because of this that Jack made poor decisions that led his ship to disaster. In this case, Jack's actions played an important role in bringing about the disaster, and he certainly failed to behave as a responsible, sober captain, but we probably shouldn't regard him as morally responsible for making his bad decisions and for the disaster that befell the ship. It would be unfair to blame Jack on account of his decisions because these decisions and their consequences would not be under his control in the right way – so they would not belong to him in the right way – for him to be held morally responsible for them.

To take another example, suppose that Captain Jack was perfectly sober and that he sailed his ship into a dangerous storm on purpose. In this case, he will bear significant causal responsibility for the consequences of his decision, and, since

he is sober, it's also likely that his decisions and their consequences will be attributable to him in a way that makes him
morally responsible for them. However, we would still want
to know *why* Jack made these decisions before confidently
making a moral assessment of his behavior. Suppose that Jack
irresponsibly sailed into the storm because he mistakenly
thought that he was equal to the task of piloting his ship
through such bad weather and that he wanted to show off
his seamanship. Here we might think that he is open to moral
blame for his bad choices. But suppose that Jack sailed into
the storm in order to outrun pirates who he reasonably
believed would kill his passengers and crew. Here, he would
still be morally responsible for his choice, but he might not
be blameworthy since his choice could well have been the
morally right one, regardless of whether it led to a bad
outcome.

Capacity Responsibility and Moral Responsibility

So far, we have seen that Jack is responsible for his ship in
the sense that he has certain powers and duties in virtue of
his role as captain and that he is causally responsible, to some
significant extent, for his ship's fate. Neither role responsibility nor causal responsibility is the same thing as moral responsibility, but some of the preceding discussion does shed light
on this latter phenomenon. For example, I noted that, if
Jack's poor choices resulted from his having been secretly
drugged, he likely would not be morally responsible for
making those choices or for the consequences that followed
from them. Similarly, your very young sister is not likely to
be morally responsible for her behavior, but your much older
brother probably would be morally responsible for his. Why
is this? As I have already suggested, part of the answer has
to do with the capacities that very young children (and
drugged sea captains) lack but that more mature (and sober)
persons typically possess.

This brings us to the portion of Hart's story in which
doctors are said to have found that Jack was "responsible for
his actions." What do doctors have to do with determining
responsibility? The answer is that medical professionals, such

as psychiatrists, are often asked (by courts, for example) to determine whether an individual had, at the time of a particular action, the capacity to deliberate about his behavior, to act on the basis of his deliberations, to understand the nature and likely consequences of his action, and so on. Agents who have these capacities – which Hart gathers under the title "capacity responsibility" – are sometimes described as responsible, or morally responsible, agents because they are, in a general way, morally and legally accountable for their behavior. In other words, when such people fall short of moral or legal standards, they are generally open to moral blame or legal punishment. Here we have come close to the heart of moral responsibility. We'll focus on the psychological capacities required for moral responsibility at several points in subsequent chapters (particularly in chapter 4).

It seems, then, that moral responsibility is crucially underwritten by the possession of powers of understanding, reasoning, and control over one's own conduct, and that those who lack these powers – infants, non-human animals, drugged sea captains – are not morally responsible for their behavior. But, again, why do these powers and capacities matter so much for moral responsibility? This is a question that will occupy much of our attention in what follows, but the basis for a partial answer was given above when I distinguished between the behavior of your seventeen-year-old brother and that of your two-year-old sister. Your brother's behavior is likely to have a significance for you that your sister's lacks because he grasps the nature of his actions and controls them in accordance with his judgments about how he has reason to behave. This makes your brother's action morally offensive to you in a way that your sister's is not, and it is therefore part of what makes your brother's behavior attributable to him in the way required for moral responsibility – and for moral blameworthiness, in particular. Because your sister lacks many of the powers and capacities that your brother possesses, her behavior will tend not to have the kind of moral significance that's relevant for blame, and that is why blaming her would be inappropriate.

Another result of your brother's more sophisticated rational powers and control over his behavior is that he could have recognized and responded to reasons for *not* engaging in certain behaviors. In other words, your brother had it in his power to avoid his bad behavior, and we might think that this possibility of avoiding bad behavior is required for genuine blameworthiness. Consider again the case in which Captain Jack is secretly drugged. We might say that Jack would not be morally responsible for the fate of his ship in this case because he would have lacked the capacity to help his ship avoid that fate. Alternatively (but relatedly), we might say that it would be unfair to blame Jack in this case because blame expresses our expectation that a person should adhere to certain standards of behavior, but it would be inappropriate to expect Jack, in his drugged state, to have behaved better than he did. Again, these are subjects that we'll explore in much more detail later.

Similar points apply in legal contexts. A person whose behavior is alien to her because she is not able to control it – because she is sleep-walking or suffering a seizure – is typically not open to criminal punishment on account of that behavior. The same is often true of criminal defendants who are unable to understand the nature or consequences of their behavior because of immaturity or severe cognitive impairment. Such impairments tend to undermine the attribution of moral fault to an agent, and in *criminal* legal cases a lack of moral fault tends to protect a defendant from liability. However, this is not necessarily true in civil cases: if I keep a dangerous animal, such as a tiger, on my property and it escapes and kills your livestock, a court may require me to provide you with compensation even if I was not at fault (morally or otherwise) for the tiger's escape. I might have taken all the precautions that could reasonably be expected of me but, if my tiger escapes, all my precautions may not protect me from civil liability. This is an instance of strict liability or liability without fault, which is a well-established principle of civil and regulatory law in many countries.

Liability without fault may be justified in civil cases – why should you have to suffer the loss of your livestock because of my tiger's rampage? – but an analogous principle seems unlikely to hold in the domain of moral responsibility (though, as we'll see in chapter 3, the phenomenon of *moral luck* may call this claim into question). And it seems to be a precondition of having and exhibiting a moral fault that an agent has the kinds of capacities described in this section.

1.2 Free Will and Determinism

As we have just seen, moral responsibility requires that people have some sort of control over how they act. This is because the behavior for which an agent is morally responsible should be attributable to him or her in a way that sustains moral assessment and moral responses such as praise and blame. But how should we characterize the sort of control required for moral responsibility? Many philosophers believe that the relevant kind of control involves possession of *free will*; they believe that people are open to moral blame, for example, only insofar as their behavior results from the exercise of their free will.

Historically, most discussions of moral responsibility have occurred in the context of debates about free will. The most prominent issue in these debates has been the compatibility of free will (and thus moral responsibility) and various forms of determinism. There are many excellent introductions to free will that treat this subject in detail, so I will not say much about it in this book. However, the issue of the compatibility of free will and determinism is so closely linked to the topic of moral responsibility that it would be *irresponsible* of me not to give readers some insight into this debate. For more detailed discussions of this topic, readers should consult texts such as Joseph Keim Campbell's excellent *Free Will* (2011), which is also part of the Polity Key Concepts in Philosophy series.

At its core, causal determinism is the thesis that, for any point in time, the state of the universe at that time (together with the laws of nature) determines, or causally necessitates, a specific future. Thus, if determinism is true, there is for each of us and for the world as a whole only one physically possible future because all the facts about the future are uniquely fixed by facts about the past (together with the laws of nature that specify how the facts about the past interact with one another).

In Robert Frost's famous poem "The Road Not Taken," the narrator – I'll call him Frost – contemplates two paths diverging in the woods. After some deliberation, Frost chooses the path "less traveled by," but he seems to have the sense that the other road was just as available to him. However, if determinism is true, then perhaps this sense of availability is an illusion. We may *feel* that we can choose the right path over the left one, chocolate over vanilla, or majoring in philosophy over majoring in physics, and we may deliberate as if these options are genuinely open to us, but, if determinism is true, there are factors over which we have no control that necessitate particular outcomes: that one goes left rather than right, chooses chocolate instead of vanilla, and so on, for every decision every person ever makes. The crucial question – or at least *a* crucial question – is whether the truth of determinism really would mean that our sense of having alternatives is illusory and that we therefore don't genuinely choose our own paths through life in the way required for moral responsibility.

So, does determinism undermine free will? It depends, of course, on what *free will* is. One commonsense approach says that having free will is just a matter of our actions being up to us, where this means having the power to perform a given action or to refrain from performing it. If this is what we think free will is, then it's easy to see why determinism might cause trouble for it. One of the most famous arguments for the conclusion that determinism is not compatible with free will is the Consequence Argument. Peter van Inwagen develops a compelling version of this argument in his book *An Essay on Free Will* (1983). Here is his summary of the basic idea behind the argument:

> If determinism is true, then our acts are the consequences of the laws of nature and events in the remote past. But it is not up to us what went on before we were born, and neither is it up to us what the laws of nature are. Therefore, the consequences of these things (including our present acts) are not up to us. (1983: 16)

Having free will means that it is up to us whether we perform an action or not. But if determinism is true, then (van Inwagen believes) whether we perform an action (or not) is *not* up to us because our performance (or non-performance) of that action is necessitated by facts about the past and the laws of nature. Thus, given the truth of determinism, our actions would be up to us in the relevant sense only if we were able to break the laws of nature or to change facts about the past – and, of course, we cannot do either of these things.

If you believe that free will (and moral responsibility) are not compatible with determinism, then you are an *incompatibilist*. An incompatibilist who believes that we nevertheless possess free will (and that determinism is therefore false) is a *libertarian*, and an incompatibilist who believes that determinism is true is a free will *skeptic* (though one can be a free will skeptic on other grounds as well). *Compatibilists*, on the other hand, believe that free will is compatible with determinism.

The Consequence Argument initially seems quite compelling, so it may seem unlikely that there is much to be said in favor of compatibilism. However, compatibilists do have responses to the Consequence Argument. They might note, for example, that the truth of determinism would not entail the view that is sometimes called *fatalism*. Fatalism – at least in one sense of the word – is the idea that specific outcomes are inescapable for us *no matter what choices we make*. In Greek mythology, an oracle told Oedipus that he was fated to murder his father and to marry his mother, and when he tried to avoid this fate, his choices merely carried him further along toward it. And if Oedipus had made different choices, these too would have led him to the same fate – that's just how fate is supposed to work. But determinism isn't necessarily like this. Certain outcomes may be determined for us, but only because we are determined to make specific choices that will lead to those outcomes. Thus, even if determinism is true, it may still be the case that determined outcomes are brought about *through our choices* and that, if we had made different choices, different outcomes would have occurred.

The distinction between determinism and fatalism can help us see a potential way in which our actions can be in our power even if determinism is true. Recall the choice with which Frost was presented. Frost took the less traveled path because he *chose* that path; if he had chosen the more traveled path, then presumably he would have taken that one. So can't we say that which path Frost took was up to him and that it was in his power to take the other path? By contrast, if Frost had chosen to teleport to his destination, then he would *not* have done so. This is just as it should be, since Frost presumably lacks power over whether he teleports to his destination: teleporting is not something he can do even if he tries to, so whether he teleports is not up to him.

These thoughts lead us to one traditional defense of the claim that free will – in the sense of being able to commit or omit a given action – is compatible with determinism. According to this approach, all we need to do is to interpret the ability to act otherwise (than we actually do) in conditional terms. (For an influential presentation of this approach, see the chapter on free will in G. E. Moore's *Ethics* [1912].) We've already applied this sort of interpretation to Frost's decision: on the condition that Frost had wanted to, or had decided to, or had chosen to take the other path, then he would have. Perhaps this is all we mean when we say that which path Frost took was up to him: for either path, if he had decided to take that path, then he would have. It seems that his actions can be up to him in this way even if determinism is true. In other words, even if the facts about the past and the laws of nature entail that Frost will take the road less traveled by, it could still be true that, *if* he had chosen the other path, he would have taken it.

How do incompatibilists respond? First of all, they can point out that, if determinism is true, Frost's decision to take the less traveled path was itself determined, which means, they will say, that he couldn't really have decided to take the other path. It might be true that, *if* Frost fulfilled a certain condition (the condition of making a different choice), he would have acted differently, but, if determinism is true, it was not possible for him to have fulfilled this condition because he was determined by antecedent causal forces to not fulfill it. Thus, determinism still seems to constitute a real limitation on the ability to do otherwise.

A related sort of objection to the conditional analysis (Lehrer 1968) has persuaded many philosophers, even many compatibilists. Suppose that Frost has a crippling case of ophidiophobia: an excessive fear of snakes. Frost's condition is such that, if he saw a snake lying on one of the paths in front of him, he would be psychologically incapable of choosing that path. Intuitively, Frost lacks the ability to take the path with the snake lying across it, but it may still be true that, *if he had chosen to take that path*, he would have done so. In this case, the conditional analysis would seem to attribute to Frost an ability that we probably don't want to say he has; so the conditional analysis appears to be faulty in some way.

However, the compatibilist is not yet finished. A different and more sophisticated – though related – compatibilist approach questions the apparently obvious claim that we can't break laws of nature. As we saw above, incompatibilists conclude from the Consequence Argument that, if determinism is true, then if a person had the ability to refrain from performing an action that she actually performed, this person must have had the ability to act contrary to the laws of nature or to change facts about the past. This follows from the fact that, if determinism is true, the past and the laws of nature ensure that a person will act just as she does. Since it is incredible to suppose that anyone could change the past or break a law of nature, the incompatibilist concludes that, if determinism is true, no one could have performed an action that they did not perform, nor could they have refrained from performing an action that they did perform.

However, as David Lewis argues in "Are We Free to Break the Laws?" ([1981] 2003), we can distinguish between a strong and a weak sense in which one may be said to break a law of nature. Frost would break a law of nature in the strong sense if he were to run down whichever path he chose faster than the speed of light. If it is a law of nature that no one can run faster than the speed of light, then Frost's act would itself violate a law of nature. Of course, laws of nature are by definition exceptionless, so no one can break a law of nature in this sense. But we might also say that a person can break a law of nature if she can perform an action that is such that, if she were to perform it, the laws of nature would have been different from what they are. For example, if it is determined (by the actual laws of nature) that Frost chooses the less traveled path, then, if he can choose the other path, he can do something that would entail that the laws of nature are not what they are. As Lewis notes, this "is not to say that anything would have been both a law and broken – that is a contradiction in terms"; instead, "something that is in fact a law, and unbroken, would have been broken, and no law" (ibid.: 123).

Now this sort of ability may still sound pretty fantastic, but Lewis didn't have anything fantastic in mind. The example that he gives is that he is able to put his hand down on his desk ([1981] 2003: 124). Can Lewis put his hand down on his desk? Of course he can (in some sense of "can"): he has the requisite muscles, nerves, and control over his body to perform this simple task. But it is also true that, if it is actually determined that Lewis will not put his hand on his desk, he will not do so, and if he did do so then the laws of nature would have to be different from those that determined that he would not do so. Still, it feels very natural to say that Lewis *can* put his hand down: it's a simple task, Lewis has a history of putting his hand up or down as the mood strikes him, and so on. So perhaps it is fair to say that he *can* put his hand on his desk *even if he certainly won't* (because the actual laws of nature make it the case that he won't). Lewis can do it – he has the general capacities required for doing it – but, if he were to do it, the laws of nature would have to be different from what they turn out to be if in fact he does not put his hand down. And perhaps all that free will requires is the ability to do otherwise understood in this sense. (Vihvelin 2011 includes a very helpful account of Lewis's argument and its relationship to the Consequence Argument.)

Some compatibilists have found Lewis's approach appealing, but incompatibilists have a ready reply: they simply insist that the ability to do otherwise that matters for free will and moral responsibility is an ability that can actually be exercised at this very moment without anything about the past or the laws of nature having to be different from what they are. According to the incompatibilist, what we want is the power to extend the *actual* past in multiple ways, not just the ability to act differently had the past or the laws been different from what they actually are. To the incompatibilist, the compatibilist's account of free will seems not to be the right sort of thing at all; it seems to be, as Immanuel Kant put it in his *Critique of Practical Reason*, "a wretched subterfuge" that substitutes something else for the thing that we really want ([1788] 1997: 80 [5:96]).

1.3   What if Determinism is False?

One of the interesting things about the free will debate is that it is not clear that the *falsity* of determinism would guarantee possession of the sort of free will that makes us morally responsible for our behavior. Once again, we can turn to Peter van Inwagen for a helpful illustration (1983: 127–8, 144). Imagine that determinism is *false* and that, as Clyde considers stealing money from a church poor box, he thinks back to the promise he made to his mother to be an honest person; he reflects on his desire to be the sort of person his mother wanted him to be and on the fact that stealing from the poor box would mean that he had broken his promise. Now suppose that these thoughts and feelings come together in such a way that Clyde refrains from stealing the money. Perhaps, as things turn out, this is his first step on the path to becoming a decent person. But note that, since we're assuming that determinism is false, Clyde's desires and reflections did not *have to* give rise to the decision to not steal.

Next, imagine that at some point in the future – after Clyde has reformed his ways and become a model citizen – God decides to "rewind" Clyde's life to the point right before he made his decision to not steal from the poor box. He is now in exactly the same position that he was in before, he has precisely the same thoughts and feelings that he originally had, and he is faced with the same choice: Should he take the money? If God lets time go forward again, what choice will Clyde make? If determinism is false, then maybe even God cannot be certain about the answer to this question. Perhaps, as van Inwagen says, "we can only wait and see" (1983: 144).

Clyde may well decide to steal the money the second time around, and this could be true even though there are no other differences between the first and second instances of his choice. If determinism is false, a set of causal inputs need not guarantee a particular outcome, so we shouldn't be too surprised that Clyde could be in exactly the same position as he was the first time around and yet make a different choice when presented with exactly the same opportunity. That's the price of indeterminism: we might know all the relevant facts about Clyde's state of mind, his moral character, and so on, but, if his choice is undetermined, not know which choice he will make because these things are not enough to ensure a certain choice. But if his decision is still up in the air even after all the relevant facts about him have been taken into account, how can the decision to steal (or to not steal) be attributed to Clyde in the right way for it to count as freely willed and for it be included in our moral assessment of him?

Reflections like these have led some people to argue that determinism is actually *necessary* for free will and moral responsibility – though this is a much less popular thesis now than it was in the early twentieth century. R. E. Hobart argues for this conclusion in his famous 1934 paper "Free Will as Involving Determination and Inconceivable Without It." (Interestingly, the author chose a pseudonym to write this widely discussed paper – his real name was Dickinson S. Miller.) Hobart argued that free will requires determinism because, in order for our actions to count as free in the right way for us to be morally responsible for them, they need to be determined by facts about ourselves – for example, by facts about our moral characters. (Hobart's essay is very suggestive but it suffers from the problematic assumption that all causation is deterministic. Philippa Foot offers decisive objections to this aspect of his view in her 1957 paper "Free Will as Involving Determinism.")

The possibility that it might be incompatible with *both* determinism and indeterminism has led some people to become skeptics about free will. However, van Inwagen is confident that we have free will and that it is incompatible with determinism; thus, he is forced to reject the argument that free will is incompatible with *in*determinism, though he admits that he cannot say exactly what is wrong with the argument described in this section (1983: 148–50). In the end, van Inwagen believes

that there is no position that one can take concerning free will that does not confront its adherent with mystery. I myself prefer the following mystery: I believe that the outcome of our deliberations about what to do is undetermined and that it is nevertheless – in some way I have no shadow of an understanding of – sometimes up to us what the outcome of these deliberations will be. (2009: 270)

As van Inwagen sees things, the skeptic and the compatibilist must tolerate even greater mysteries.

1.4 The Principle of Alternate Possibilities and Frankfurt-Style Compatibilism

The varieties of compatibilism described so far aim to establish the compatibility of free will and determinism by showing that we can have the ability to do otherwise even if determinism is true. It's typically assumed that, in establishing the compatibility of free will and determinism, we also establish the compatibility of moral responsibility and determinism. However, it's possible to argue for the compatibility of moral responsibility and determinism more directly by showing that moral responsibility does not require the ability to do otherwise. If this is true, then determinism does not exclude moral responsibility simply by excluding the type of free will that involves the ability to do otherwise (though determinism might exclude moral responsibility for other reasons, as we will see in §3.4).

In his paper "Alternate Possibilities and Moral Responsibility" ([1969] 1988a), Harry Frankfurt offered an influential compatibilist argument along the lines just described. This argument employs a supposed counter-example to the Principle of Alternate Possibilities (PAP), which claims that a person is morally responsible for what she does only if she could have done otherwise. The counter-example Frankfurt proposes is meant to be a case in which a person is morally responsible for an action even though she could not have avoided performing it.

Many other philosophers have devised cases based on Frankfurt's original. What these cases have in common is that they feature a person – call him Jones – who is considering whether to perform a certain action, and a second person – call him Black – who wants, and who is able, to make sure that Jones performs the action in question. However, it turns out that Black does not have to intervene to get what he wants: Jones acts the way Black wants him to without Black doing anything. Since Black doesn't actually intervene in the process leading to Jones's action, Black is called a "counter-factual intervener."

As I said, many philosophers have offered examples along these lines. We'll consider a fairly recent one from John Martin Fischer, one of the most prominent contemporary defenders of Frankfurt's sort of compatibilism. The example is set in 2008, just prior to the US presidential election in which the Democratic candidate, Barack Obama, defeated John McCain, the Republican candidate:

> Because he dares to hope that the Democrats finally have a good chance of winning the White House...Black...has secretly inserted a chip in Jones's brain that enables Black to monitor and control Jones's activities. Black can exercise this control through a sophisticated computer that he has pro-grammed so that, among other things, it monitors Jones's voting behavior. If Jones were to show any inclination to vote for McCain...then the computer, through the chip in Jones's brain, would intervene to assure that he actually decides to vote for Obama and does so vote. But if Jones decides on his own to vote for Obama...the computer does nothing but continue to monitor – without affecting – the goings-on in Jones's head. (Fischer 2010: 316)

Now suppose that Black's computer never receives any indication that Jones is inclining toward McCain and that Jones ends up voting for Obama on his own and for his own reasons. As Frankfurt put it in his original example, "Black never has to show his hand because [Jones], for reasons of his own, decides to perform and does perform the very action Black wants him to perform" ([1969] 1988a: 7). Frankfurt and Fischer argue that examples such as these count against PAP because, even though Jones cannot do otherwise than to vote for Obama, he seems morally responsible for his behav-ior. And why wouldn't he be responsible? After all, Jones's action was brought about in the normal way. Of course, it's not normal to have someone like Black ready to step in and take control of your behavior, but Black didn't actually do anything to Jones: Jones acted for his own reasons in the way that people normally do, so he's morally responsible for his action.

However, many authors resist the conclusion that Frankfurt cases – as these examples are often called – show that access to alternatives is irrelevant for moral responsibility. Some of these authors argue that the examples don't give us cases in which access to alternatives is entirely excluded. Think back to Fischer's case. Didn't Jones have at least the following alternative: while he performed his action on his own, he might instead have performed the action because Black forced him to? Similarly, while the workings of Jones's brain gave no indication to Black's computer that Jones was forming an inclination to vote for McCain, it seems that such an indication might have been given. So perhaps Fischer's example hasn't entirely excluded Jones's access to alternatives, in which case it does not provide us with evidence that such access is irrelevant to moral responsibility. For an objection to Frankfurt cases along these lines, see van Inwagen (1983: 166–80).

One response to this criticism – a response urged by Fischer himself – is that, even if the alternatives just described are present, they don't seem to be alternatives that could be relevant to moral responsibility. Note that, if Jones had taken the alternative path described above, then he would certainly *not* be exercising the sort of free will that is supposed to be required for moral responsibility because, in the alternative scenario, Black would have been in control of his behavior. Fischer says, "it is highly implausible to suppose that it is *in virtue* of the existence of such an alternative possibility that Jones is morally responsible" ([2003] 2006a: 45). That is, it's implausible to suppose that the story of Jones voting for Obama for his own reasons goes from being one of non-responsibility to one of responsibility only if Jones had the alternative of voting for Obama under circumstances in which he would *not* have been morally responsible. And if the alternative in question doesn't seem relevant to Jones's moral responsibility, then perhaps its presence in Fischer's example is consistent with his claim that access to alternatives is not necessary for moral responsibility.

But incompatibilists might also wonder how Black can *know* that, if his computer receives an indication of one sort (but not of another sort), Jones will vote for Obama. Perhaps the only way to explain this is to say that Black's computer detects a causally deterministic process in Jones's brain that will unavoidably lead him to vote for Obama. However, if Fischer's example is to be of use to compatibilists, then it needs to be clear that Jones is morally responsible for voting for Obama even though he couldn't have done otherwise, and, if Jones's action was causally determined, incompatibilists are not likely to agree that he is morally responsible for it.

It seems, then, that a proponent of Frankfurt cases faces the following dilemma (Widerker [1995] 2003). Either Jones's behavior is determined or it is not. If Jones's behavior is determined, then the example doesn't show incompatibilists that access to alternatives is not necessary for moral responsibility because incompatibilists will not agree that Jones is morally responsible. On the other hand, if Jones's behavior is not determined, then incompatibilists might agree that he is responsible for voting for Obama, but they won't agree that he lacked access to alternatives (since, if determinism is false, Jones might have done otherwise). Therefore, according to incompatibilist critics, the example doesn't show what it is meant to: it either fails to be an example featuring moral responsibility or it fails to be an example in which access to alternatives is absent.

1.5 The Importance of Acting for One's Own Reasons

A great deal of ingenuity has gone into developing more elaborate versions of Frankfurt cases in an effort to evade objections like those just described (see, for example, Mele and Robb 1998; Hunt 2000; Pereboom 2001: 18–22). I won't go into the details of these revised examples. Instead, I want to focus on what I take to be the core of Frankfurt's position in a way that will frame some of the issues about moral responsibility that we'll engage in later chapters.

In his 1969 paper, Frankfurt concedes that people who tell us that they could not have done otherwise are often not morally responsible for their behavior. Why is this an effective excuse? Frankfurt says that it is "because we assume that what they tell us serves to explain why they did what they did" ([1969] 1988a: 9). For example, if a person tells you that she could not have done otherwise than to commit some act because she was driven to do it by an irresistible compulsion or by a coercive threat, then the factors that made it so that the person could not have done otherwise also play a crucial role in explaining why she did what she did.

But why is a person excused when factors such as compulsion or coercion explain her behavior? Here is one answer. If a person's behavior is explained by the fact that she was subject to an overwhelming compulsion, then her behavior is out of her control in the sense that the expected link between the agent's actions and her desires and judgments has been severed: instead of acting as she wanted to act or as she judged that she ought to act, she acted compulsively. In such a case, the agent's behavior may not belong to her – it may not express who she is and where she stands – in the right way to support an ascription of moral responsibility.

A related point applies to cases of coercion. Suppose that Bonnie helps Clyde rob a bank because Clyde threatened to kill her if she didn't. Additionally, suppose that you believe that, given Clyde's threat, it was reasonable and permissible for Bonnie to do what he demanded. In this case, Bonnie can in one sense be said to have acted as seemed best to her, but we probably wouldn't say that she robbed the bank of her own accord. Instead, we might say that Clyde's threat explains Bonnie's behavior because *he gave her no choice*. (Of course, Clyde didn't make other choices literally impossible for Bonnie; he just gave her overwhelmingly good reason not to defy him.) Perhaps, since Bonnie's action followed from a choice of hers, we would say that she is morally responsible for so acting but, if we agree that her choice does not reflect poorly on her, we won't regard her as blameworthy.

In the cases just described, the following claims appear to be true:

(i) the agents in these cases are excused from moral responsibility (or at least from moral blame);

(ii) the agents in these cases could not have done otherwise (or at least they could not reasonably have been expected to do otherwise);

(iii) the facts that explain why these agents could not have done otherwise (or could not have been expected to do otherwise) also explain why they acted as they did.

Note, however, that, while the agents in these cases are excused from blame and they could not have done otherwise, they don't seem to be excused *just because* they could not have done otherwise. What really seems to do the excusing work is that the agents in these cases are, in different ways, not acting for their own reasons or of their own accord – or at least they are not doing so in ways that reflect poorly on them. Frankfurt's insight – and what Frankfurt cases illustrate – is that, while scenarios in which people cannot do otherwise are often cases in which they do not act of their own accord (which is what happens in the compulsion and coercion cases above), the fact that a person cannot avoid a particular action does not by itself entail that she fails to act of her own accord.

Another way to make this point is to emphasize, as Frankfurt has more recently, "that making an action unavoidable *is not the same thing* as bringing it about that the action is performed" (2006: 340). The point of his examples, Frankfurt now says, is to draw our attention to this conceptual distinction and not necessarily to give us scenarios in which every sort of alternative is excluded for an agent (ibid.: 339–40). Keeping this distinction in mind leads us to focus on the factors that actually explain a person's behavior rather than on whether she might have done otherwise, and Frankfurt thinks that this shift in focus naturally loosens the grip that PAP can otherwise have on us. The crucial thing for moral responsibility "is not," says Frankfurt, "what actions the person could have performed but how the action that he did perform was effectively brought about" (ibid.: 340). Appreciating this difference makes it easy to see that what really counts is not whether an action was avoidable but in what way it came to be that the action was performed. When a person acts for reasons of his own, and is guided entirely by his own beliefs and preferences, the question of whether he could have done something else instead is quite irrelevant to an assessment of his moral responsibility. Analyses purporting to show that agents do invariably have alternatives are simply not to the point... (Ibid.)

The most basic commitment of Frankfurt-style compatibilism is, then, something like the following: moral responsibility is compatible with an inability to do otherwise because such an inability is compatible with a person acting for her own reasons and based on her own preferences, beliefs, judgments, and so on. This plausible conceptual point is largely untouched by the criticisms of Frankfurt cases that we saw in the last section. Instead, what Frankfurt's incompatibilist critics would need to show is that agents act for their own reasons (in the way required for moral responsibility) only if determinism is false.

Now it may well be true that determinism threatens our ability to act for our own reasons. At any rate, if determinism is true, there are causal determinants prior to our reasons, preferences, and beliefs that bring about our actions and that make it so that we cannot do otherwise. So why not say that it is these causal determinants that *really* explain our behavior if determinism is true? Frankfurt raised a concern along these lines in his original paper ([1969] 1988a: 9–10). His response was that, even if we can explain a person's behavior by referencing the way causal determinants excluded alternatives for her, it does not follow that the agent acted as she did *only* because she could not have done otherwise.

The idea can perhaps be put this way: insofar as external causal forces explain our behavior, they often do so by exploiting our capacities as judgers, deliberators, desirers, and choosers, and not by circumventing or overriding these capacities. John Martin Fischer captures this important point this way:

Note that even if causal determinism obtains, invocation of prior states of the world plus the natural laws cannot explain our behavior and its upshots without *also* explaining that *we make a certain sort of contribution to them*. That is, the prior conditions and laws of nature explain what happens only by also explaining that we make a certain sort of contribution – that our deliberations have a certain character, for example. The very factors that explain what happens cannot explain the way the world actually unfolds without *also* explaining that we make a certain sort of contribution through (for example) our unhindered deliberations. ([2002] 2006b: 135)

Of course, the incompatibilist might reply that, if we are *determined* to make certain contributions to the causal scene, these contributions are not really our own in the right way for us to be morally responsible for the resulting behavior (we'll see this sort of objection in chapter 3). However, I'll set this objection aside for the moment and conclude this section by noting that Fischer and Frankfurt are focusing on something that even incompatibilists can agree is important for moral responsibility. Whether we are compatibilists or incompatibilists, and even after the problem of determinism has been set aside, we will still often want to know *why* someone did what she did when it comes to assessing her moral responsibility. We will want to know whether she acted for reasons that she regarded as supporting the course she took, whether she acted as she wanted to act, and so on.

1.6 Conclusion

In this chapter I distinguished various ways in which talk of responsibility is used and began to identify some of the central elements of *moral* responsibility (particularly in the section on what H. L. A. Hart calls capacity responsibility). However, most of this chapter was spent on the relationship between free will and determinism; this debate will largely recede into the background in what follows (with notable exceptions, such as §3.2). For the most part, the focus in the following chapters will be on issues like those raised in the closing paragraph of the last section and in the quotation from Fischer that preceded it – in other words, issues about moral responsibility that would remain even if the problem of determinism were set aside. These issues include questions about the general character of ascriptions of moral responsibility and of praise and blame, questions about what kind of contribution an agent must make to an action (independently of the issue of determinism) if she is to be morally responsible for it, and questions about what factors (besides determinism) might be thought to impair an agent's ability to make these contributions.

1.7 Further Reading

I have already mentioned Joseph K. Campbell's (2011) introductory text on free will; readers will find a similar book by Robert Kane (2005) helpful as well. Alfred Mele (2014) offers an accessible philosophical critique of recent research from psychology and neuroscience bearing on free will. There are a number of important, non-introductory monographs that serious students of the subject will want to read: these include Randolph Clarke's *Libertarian Accounts of Free Will* (2003), John Martin Fischer and Mark Ravizza's *Responsibility and Control* (1998), Robert Kane's *The Significance of Free Will* (1996), Alfred Mele's *Autonomous Agents* (1995), Derk Pereboom's *Living Without Free Will* (2001), Peter van Inwagen's *An Essay on Free Will* (1983), and Susan Wolf's *Freedom Within Reason* (1990), among others. There are also many valuable collections of essays on free will, among them Russell and Deery (2013), Watson (2003), and Widerker and McKenna (2003). These recent anthologies are nicely supplemented by older collections (if one can find them) such as those edited by Berofsky (1966), Dworkin (1970a), and Hook (1961). The *Stanford Encyclopedia of Philosophy* is an excellent online philosophical resource, and it includes a number of fine essays on the topics of this chapter: Clarke and Capes (2014), McKenna and Coates (2015), O'Connor (2014), and Vihvelin (2011). The topic of omissions is a fascinating one that went largely unnoticed in this chapter. Readers will find much of value on this subject in Randolph Clarke's recent book *Omissions: Agency, Metaphysics, and Responsibility* (2014), as well as in the fifth chapter of Fischer and Ravizza's *Responsibility and Control* (1998).

2
Approaches to Moral Responsibility

As I noted in the Introduction, we want a theory of moral responsibility, and particularly of blameworthiness, because we would like to have an account of when our responsibility practices are justified. Thus, a theory of moral responsibility should give us a compelling and consistent story about when and why a person is open to praise and blame and of what we are doing when we engage in these practices. We may look to such theories particularly in difficult or borderline cases in which common sense and common practice are not the best guides. On the other hand, theories of responsibility are often judged by how well their results conform to common sense, and it's frequently regarded as a bad thing when a theory yields conclusions that conflict with widely held intuitions about when a person is open to praise or blame. Still, we should – and we will, in the next chapter – take seriously the possibility that we may uncover theoretical grounds for rejecting some (and perhaps a great deal) of our pre-theoretical conclusions about moral responsibility.

In this chapter, I will describe a few different ways of thinking about moral responsibility and of accounting for our practices of blaming, praising, and excusing others for their behavior. I will start with an approach that used to be quite popular but that has now largely fallen out of favor.

2.1   Forward-Looking Approaches to Moral Responsibility

One way of developing an account of moral responsibility is to think about the point of our practices of praise and blame. Why do we engage in these activities? It's clear that part of the reason we praise and blame is to encourage others to adopt certain forms of behavior and to discourage them from acting in other ways. So perhaps a person is morally responsible for her behavior just insofar as praising or blaming her has a good chance of encouraging or discouraging different kinds of behavior. Such approaches are said to be *forward-looking* or *consequentialist* because they focus on whether our acts of praise and blame are likely to bring about certain consequences.

These theories of moral responsibility are often embedded in a larger consequentialist moral outlook according to which actions are right or wrong depending on whether they promote, or tend to promote, good or bad consequences. In the end, it is the tenets of this broader consequentialist perspective that provide a lot of the support for forward-looking accounts of moral responsibility. In other words, if one accepts consequentialism as one's moral theory, the forward-looking approach to moral responsibility will seem much more natural than it might otherwise. Unfortunately, a discussion of the merits of consequentialism would take us well beyond the scope of this book.

Moritz Schlick advances a forward-looking perspective on moral responsibility in "When is a Man Responsible?," a once widely anthologized chapter from his 1930 book *Fragen der Ethik* (*Problems in Ethics*). Schlick regarded philosophy's recurring interest in the compatibility of determinism and free will as something of an embarrassment. According to Schlick, the problem of free will was nothing more than a "pseudo-problem" that had long since been dealt with by the great eighteenth-century Scottish philosopher David Hume, among others (Schlick [1930] 1966: 54). The classic reply to his pseudo-problem claim is by C. A. Campbell ([1951] 1966).

The appearance of conflict between freedom and determinism arises, Schlick claims, from a tendency to assume that *descriptive* natural laws (of the sort invoked by determinists) function like *prescriptive* civil laws. Civil laws compel us through the threat of punishment to act in law-abiding ways regardless of whether we want to do so. But deterministic natural laws would not, if they obtained, function this way: while determinism might make our actions inevitable, it would not force us to act contrary to, and independently of, our own motives and desires. This means that the truth of determinism would not have the same moral significance as the discovery that a person's behavior resulted from external coercive pressures such as threats of violence. For Schlick, "[f]reedom means the opposite of compulsion," and a person "is compelled or unfree when he is hindered from without... when he is locked up, or chained, or when someone forces him at the point of a gun to do what otherwise he would not do" ([1930] 1966: 59). Since the truth of determinism would not mean that people are compelled in this way, it follows for Schlick that freedom – at least of a certain sort – is compatible with determinism (ibid.).

The kind of freedom that Schlick regards as compatible with determinism is constituted by the ability to acquire motives and to act on them. This freedom is sufficient for moral responsibility as far as Schlick is concerned because judgments of moral responsibility are, on his view, simply judgments about whom to punish or reward. And, for Schlick, people are open to punishment or reward if the prospect of these things provides them with motives to act in desirable ways. As he sees it, "[p]unishment is concerned only with the institution of causes, of *motives* of conduct"; it's purely "an educative measure" aiming to "prevent the wrongdoer from repeating the act" and "to prevent others from committing a similar act" ([1930] 1966: 60). Thus, "[t]he question of who is responsible is the question concerning the *correct point of application of the motive....* It is a matter only of knowing who is to be punished or rewarded..." (ibid.: 61).

It's worth noting that, while Schlick's compatibilism is comparatively primitive, it does overlap in an important respect with the more sophisticated variety of compatibilism that we saw offered by Harry Frankfurt in the last chapter. Both views insist that whether someone is able to act on her own motives, and for her own reasons, is crucial for moral responsibility. The problem with Schlick's view is that it accounts for the importance of this ability solely in terms of how this feature of human beings can be exploited to get better subsequent behavior out of them. Most contemporary authors regard this position as missing something important about the point, and the character, of our moral responsibility practices. I'll say more about this criticism in a moment.

In his important paper "Free Will, Praise, and Blame" ([1961] 2003), J. J. C. Smart develops a view similar to Schlick's. Smart's approach involves a distinction between blame and "dispraise." To praise or dispraise people is to grade their behavior (or their attributes) positively or negatively against a relevant standard. We may praise and dispraise both the moral and non-moral aspects of a person:

> Just as we may praise or dispraise…a footballer for his fleetness or slowness of foot, a lecturer in philosophy for his intelligence or lack of intelligence, and a writer for clarity or obscurity, so naturally enough, we may praise or dispraise a man for his honesty or dishonesty, truthfulness or untruthfulness, kindness or unkindness and so on. (Ibid.: 70)

Since praise and dispraise merely assess behavior in positive or negative terms, they do not entail that people are responsible for their behavior. However, *blame*, on Smart's account, does entail responsibility: blame "is just a grading [dispraise, in other words] plus an ascription of responsibility" (ibid.). And people are responsible for their behavior, according to Smart, if they would have omitted that behavior under appropriate circumstances – for example, under circumstances in which they were provided with motives (as Schlick would say) for avoiding that behavior. Thus, a blameworthy agent is a person who performs a bad action – a dispraiseworthy action – that she could have avoided, where *could have avoided* means that the person would have avoided the action if she had taken herself to have good reason to do so.

To illustrate his view, Smart tells the story of Tommy:

> Suppose Tommy at school does not do his homework. If the schoolmaster thinks that this is because Tommy is really very stupid, then it is silly of him to abuse Tommy, to cane him or to threaten him. This would be sensible only if it were the case that this sort of treatment made stupid boys intelligent. ... The schoolmaster says, then, that Tommy is not to blame, he just *could not* have done his homework. Now suppose that the reason why Tommy did not do his homework is that he was lazy: perhaps he had just settled down to do it when some other boy tempted him to come out and climb a tree. In such a case the schoolmaster will hold Tommy responsible, and he will say that Tommy could have done his homework. ([1961] 2003: 68)

In the version of the story in which Tommy is simply incapable of doing his homework, we still accurately assess his performance as poor – that is, we dispraise him – but we do not blame him. Presumably, what this means is that we refrain from following up our dispraise of Incapable-Tommy with a sanction (such as the "abuse" and "threats" that Smart mentions). We refrain from these sanctions because they would be useless as a means of getting Incapable-Tommy to do better next time. However, in the version of the example in which Tommy is lazy, he is responsible for not doing his homework because his failure stems from a choice that he would have omitted under different circumstances. (For example, Lazy-Tommy might have completed his homework if he had been worried that he would be caned for not completing it.) Hence we do not merely grade Lazy-Tommy's performance as poor, we also blame him. That is, we provide him with an incentive – again, some type of sanction or other treatment that Tommy would like to avoid – to help ensure that he makes a different choice next time. Of course, it is not the presently applied sanction that gets Tommy to make a better choice next time so much as the threat that another sanction will follow upon his making another poor choice. The present sanction helps to make this threat credible.

Smart's account is, like Schlick's, forward-looking: it justifies particular instances of praise or blame in terms of their likely beneficial consequences. One problem with this sort of view is that, if our practices of praise and blame are justified solely by their propensity for bringing about certain consequences, praise and blame will be justifiable in very counter-intuitive contexts. For example, there may be cases in which *praising* a *bad* actor will maximize future instances of good behavior (on the part of the praised agent or on the part of others), and in such cases it would be appropriate to praise the bad actor and inappropriate to blame him. For this reason, Smart says, in "An Outline of a Utilitarian System of Ethics," that a person should "learn to control his acts of praise and dispraise, thus perhaps concealing his approval of an action when he thinks that the expression of such approval might have bad effects, and perhaps even praising actions of which he does not really approve" (1973: 49–50).

Smart's position here follows from his commitment to the consequentialist view "that the rightness or wrongness of an action depends only on the total goodness or badness of its consequences, i.e. on the effect of the action on the welfare of all human beings (or perhaps all sentient beings)" (1973: 4). If we agree with Smart that we ought generally to act so as to increase the total amount of good in the world, then we will try to apply this standard to our acts of praise and blame as much as to any of our other actions. This can lead to instances of blame that may appear unjust, but from Smart's perspective these acts will be permissible (or even required) if – on balance and all things considered – they lead to the best available outcomes.

If, however, you think that praise and blame ought to be more closely tied to the rightness or wrongness (or goodness or badness) of a person's actions, then you will find a view like Smart's unappealing. You may feel, for example, that, while it would be *useful* to blame a particular person, it might still be unfair to do so because the person has done nothing wrong or because she has an excuse for any wrong that she did. Assessing acts of praise and blame in terms of their consequences, you might say, is simply to measure these things by the wrong metric. (Of course, Smart might reply that he is not trying to describe our actual practices of praise and blame but is instead telling us what our practices *ought to be*.)

Accounts like Smart's and Schlick's also strike many readers as presenting implausibly sterile and disengaged versions of our moral responsibility practices. These accounts largely ignore the deep interpersonal significance that our practices have for us, regarding them merely as tools for achieving certain ends. However, praise and blame seem to be important not just because of what they can do, but also because of what they mean for us and for our relations with one another. Smart and Schlick know, of course, that people dislike being blamed – that's what makes blame such a useful tool! – but they have little to say about *why* we dislike it so much. Similarly, both have little of value to say about the offended emotional tone that usually characterizes blame. Smart simply dismisses this aspect of our practices as the "quasi-superstitious" result of bad metaphysics – at least when it is not mere pretense justified on consequentialist grounds (1973: 53). However, as we shall see in the next section, it is possible to provide a richer account of moral responsibility – to say much more, for example, about the emotional content of blame and our aversion to being its target – without falling into the kind of "metaphysical nonsense" that Smart derides (ibid.: 54). (See Pereboom 2014 for a different sort of forward-looking approach to moral responsibility that avoids some of the challenges faced by Schlick's and Smart's accounts.)

2.2 The Reactive Attitudes Approach

In contrast to the approaches taken by Smart and Schlick, P. F. Strawson, in his landmark essay "Freedom and Resentment," first published in 1963, is deeply concerned with our interpersonal relationships and the way that our practices of holding one another morally responsible are shaped by these relationships. The feature of our relationships – and of our responsibility practices – that most interests Strawson is our tendency to respond to other people with a set of *reactive attitudes* on account of how they have treated us. These attitudes include such things as "gratitude, resentment, forgiveness, love, and hurt feelings" (Strawson [1963] 1993: 48). As the title of Strawson's paper suggests, the attitude of *resentment* often takes center stage. On Strawson's view, the best way to understand moral responsibility, excuse, forgiveness, and related phenomena is to consider the contexts in which attitudes such as resentment arise and the contexts that tend to calm or inhibit these attitudes.

Strawson characterizes his approach as an attempt to bridge the distance between "optimists" and "pessimists" about the prospects of reconciling moral responsibility and determinism. Strawson's optimist is basically a compatibilist in the mold of Smart or Schlick; that is, one who justifies our moral responsibility practices by reference to their usefulness as tools of social control and moral education. Strawson's pessimist (a libertarian of the sort described in §1.2) finds this consequentialist approach incomplete, cramped, and shallow and believes that a truer and richer account of moral responsibility must appeal to a sort of free will that is incompatible with determinism.

Strawson agrees with the pessimist that views like Smart's and Schlick's are incomplete: there really is more to be said in favor of our responsibility practices than that they are useful in achieving certain goals. However, Strawson does not believe that we need to appeal to a particular conception of free will in order to make up for the deficits in the optimist's account. Instead, we need only to understand the function and internal logic of attitudes such as resentment, for "it is," says Strawson, "just these attitudes themselves which fill the gap in the optimist's account" ([1963] 1993: 64). The idea is that, when we understand the role these attitudes play and how they are naturally elicited and inhibited, we will see that our practices of praise, blame, forgiveness, and so on, can get along just fine without appealing to the sort of free will the pessimist has in mind.

For Strawson, the animating force behind our responsibility practices is our intense interest in the *quality of will* toward us that other people express through their behavior. We care, for example, about "whether the actions of other people – and particularly of *some* other people – reflect attitudes towards us of goodwill, affection, or esteem on the one hand or contempt, indifference, or malevolence on the other" ([1963] 1993: 49). Indeed, we normally impose on others a *demand* that they treat us with a certain degree of respect and good will, or at least with an absence of ill will. We demand, in other words, that people treat us with due regard, and when this demand is not met we typically feel resentment. A reactive attitude such as resentment is, then, a way of expressing the demand for due regard and of bringing this demand to bear in our relationships with others. In fact, according to Strawson, "the making of the demand [for due regard] *is* the proneness to" attitudes such as resentment (ibid.: 63); that is, we impose the demand for regard on someone just insofar as we are liable to feel resentment toward that person when our demand is flouted or ignored. More broadly, to regard other people as generally morally responsible for their behavior is to regard them as generally open to the interpersonal demand for due regard and thus as generally appropriate targets for positive and negative reactive attitudes.

Resentment is Strawson's primary example of a *personal* reactive attitude. These are attitudes that we are liable to feel toward others on account of how their behavior affects *us*: resentment is what I feel when I hold someone morally responsible for behavior that seems to express ill will or disregard toward *me*. But we also hold people morally responsible for their behavior toward *others*. Strawson says that, in this case, we feel "sympathetic or vicarious or impersonal or disinterested or generalized analogues of the reactive attitudes" ([1963] 1993: 56). He calls the vicarious analogue of resentment *indignation*: it is the attitude that is aroused when someone fails to show due regard for the interests and welfare of a third party. There are also reflexive or "self-reactive" attitudes such as shame and the feeling of being "bound or obliged" to perform, or to refrain from performing, certain actions (ibid.: 57). These last are expressions of the moral demands that we impose on ourselves or that we feel to be rightly imposed on us by others.

To see the significance that a person's orientation toward us has for our relations with that person, think about how you would respond to an injury that was done to you accidentally as compared to a physically identical injury that was done to you deliberately. Suppose that you are standing on a crowded subway and that someone – Bonnie, let's say – gives you a hard shove from behind. From the standpoint of any physical harm you suffer, it won't matter whether the shove was intentional, but your emotional responses will likely be very sensitive to whether you believe there was some intention behind the shove and what you take that intention to have been. Bonnie might have shoved you only because she lost her balance as a result of being jostled by someone else, or she might have been pushing you out of the way to get at the free seat that just opened up beside you.

The difference between these two explanations will likely matter to you a great deal. In the case of an intentional shove you would probably take a degree of offense, and feel a degree of resentment, that would not be appropriate in the case of the unintentional shove. This is because in the former case, but not in the latter, the person's behavior seems to betray a lack of awareness of, or concern for, your legitimate interest in not being pushed around at the convenience of others. Of course, such a lack of concern isn't always indicated by an intentional shove. A person might intentionally push you out of the way of an oncoming car, but this would not indicate a lack of concern for your welfare and would not normally be grounds for resentment; in fact, a feeling of gratitude might be the appropriate response. Furthermore, someone can disregard your interests in an offensive way without *intentionally* doing anything. Suppose that Clyde absentmindedly steps on your foot. The fact that he wasn't exercising greater intentional control over his actions might contribute to the impression that he has an objectionably low degree of concern for how his actions affect the people around him.

If Bonnie accidently shoves you (because she has lost her balance), or justifiably shoves you (because she was pushing you out of the way of traffic), it would be inappropriate to resent her because, despite initial appearances, her behavior would not indicate the kind of ill will or disregard that makes resentment an apt response. Bonnie's behavior, though perhaps initially unwelcome, was compatible with her observance of the demand for due moral regard, and this should inhibit or diminish resentment. As Strawson notes, we point to considerations like these when we say things like: " 'He didn't mean to', 'He hadn't realized', 'He didn't know'" and also " 'He had to do it', 'It was the only way', 'They left him no alternative', etc." ([1963] 1993: 50). Though Strawson doesn't call the considerations he cites *excuses*, it is a convenient and commonly applied term in this context. When the person who shoved you explains that she was pushed, she is offering you an excuse: she is giving you a reason to withhold blame and the negative reactive attitudes that play such an important role in our blaming practices.

When a person is excused from blame in the way just described, we need not revise our judgment that he is a generally morally responsible agent and generally a proper target for the reactive attitudes. As Strawson puts it, excusing considerations

> do not invite us to see the *agent* as other than a fully responsible agent. They invite us to see the *injury* as one for which he was not fully, or at all, responsible. They do not suggest that the agent is in any way an inappropriate object of that kind of demand for goodwill or regard which is reflected in our ordinary reactive attitudes. ([1963] 1993: 50–1)

However, other considerations *are* in tension with the demand for good will and therefore invite a more thoroughgoing suspension of the reactive attitudes. Agents to whom these considerations apply are often said to be *exempt* from blame, though, again, Strawson does not himself use this term. Exempting considerations don't lead us to revise our judgment about an agent's behavior so much as to revise our judgment about *the agent* himself on account of his psychological abnormality or immaturity. Of such agents, we say things like: " 'He's only a child', 'He's a hopeless schizophrenic', 'His mind has been systematically perverted', 'That's purely compulsive behaviour on his part' "; we view such agents as "warped or deranged" or as the product of "peculiarly unfortunate... formative circumstances" (Strawson [1963] 1993, 51–2). Because of impairments and incapacities such as these, the person in question is different from psychologically normal adults in ways that show him to be an inappropriate subject for our moral demands and hence an inappropriate target of our reactive attitudes. Such an agent is not "seen as a morally responsible agent, as a term of moral relationships, as a member of the moral community" (ibid.: 59).

Strawson says a different exempting condition is indicated when we say that a person acting under unusual stress "wasn't himself" ([1963] 1993: 51). His point here isn't entirely clear, but perhaps he has something like this in mind. Suppose you are normally on friendly terms with Bonnie but she is unaccountably rude to you one day. You learn later that she recently lost her job or that her beloved pet just died. It may seem inappropriate in such a case to enforce the demand for due regard on Bonnie and to resent her for her failure to meet it. Part of the explanation might be that Bonnie's behavior seems to be less than fully her own insofar as it can be attributed to the misfortunes that have befallen her rather than to her normal temperament and patterns of judgment. As Strawson puts it (in a somewhat obscure passage): "We shall not feel resentment against the man he is for the action done by the man he is not;...We normally have to deal with him under normal stresses; so we shall not feel towards him... [when he acts under abnormal stresses], as we should... [when he acts] under normal stresses" (ibid.).

Insofar as we regard a person as exempt from the demand for due regard (and from resentment and other reactive attitudes), we take up toward this person what Strawson calls an "objective attitude." In taking up this attitude, we may view a person as "an object of social policy," as a candidate for "treatment," as something "to be managed or handled or cured or trained," but we won't see him as a potential partner in the kinds of relationships where moral demands and personally engaged reactive attitudes have their home ([1963] 1993: 52). Such a person is simply not the sort of agent whose behavior can have the kind of significance or meaning for us that would make moral demands and reactive attitudes appropriate.

Strawson allows that, even in the case of normal adults, we have access to something like the objective attitude. We can, for a time at least, view normal agents mainly as objects of policy and consider our interactions with them largely in terms of how to achieve various ends. However, Strawson claims that we cannot permanently adopt an objective perspective on the behavior of others (as Schlick and Smart would perhaps have us do): the reactive attitudes come to us too easily and are too intertwined with our way of life to be given up. And, even if we *could* give up the reactive attitudes, Strawson suggests that we would have little reason to choose such an altered form of life – a form of life that he regards as impoverished and perhaps as not recognizably human ([1963] 1993: 60).

Strawson argues that the truth of determinism in particular would give us no reason to question our moral responsibility practices and to give up moral sentiments such as resentment. After all, even if determinism were true, this would not entail that everyone always falls under either an excusing or an exempting condition: it would not entail that no one ever expresses ill will through their behavior or that everyone is psychologically abnormal in a way that makes ordinary moral relationships impossible (Strawson [1963] 1993: 53–4; for astute criticisms of Strawson's claim here, see Russell 1992: 298–301). More generally, Strawson doubts that any theoretical discovery could oblige us to give up the style of personal relationship that involves vulnerability to the reactive attitudes:

> The human commitment to participation in ordinary interpersonal relationship is, I think, too thoroughgoing and deeply rooted for us to take seriously the thought that a general theoretical conviction might so change our world that, in it, there were no longer any such things as interpersonal relationships as we normally understand them; and being involved in interpersonal relationships as we normally understand them precisely is being exposed to the range of reactive attitudes and feelings that is in question. ([1963] 1993: 54)

I'll conclude this section by noting that Strawson's approach provides an important element that was missing from Harry Frankfurt's influential compatibilist theory described in the last chapter. Frankfurt notes that we care whether a person has acted for her own reasons (and that a person's doing so is compatible with determinism), but in Strawson's theory we can find an account of *why* we care about this, of why we care so much about whether a person's actions are explained by her preferences and her reflections on what she has reason to do. We care about these things because, when a person's behavior is explained in this way, it tells us something about how that person is oriented toward us and how she values our needs and interests. For example, if Bonnie knowingly injures you in order to achieve some unimportant goal, then this can tell you something about how she weighs your welfare in comparison with her own interests. In such a case, you might resent Bonnie because her action expresses an objectionable disregard for something that, by your lights, ought not to be considered so lightly.

2.3 Critiquing the Reactive Attitudes Approach

Strawson's "Freedom and Resentment" has been extremely influential for subsequent theorizing about moral responsibility, particularly in its emphasis on the role of the negative reactive attitudes and on the way our actions express morally relevant qualities of will. It has, for example, become common to think of expressions of resentment as the primary instance of moral blame and to conceive of blameworthiness largely in terms of an agent being an appropriate target of resentment (often because of the quality of will revealed through the agent's action). The editors of a recent anthology on blame describe Strawson's paper as the "founding document of contemporary work on blame" (Coates and Tognazzini 2013a: 4). This strikes me as an accurate assessment, and Strawson's essay continues to play an important role in framing the debate for work on blame and on moral responsibility more generally.

But Strawson's theory has also encountered criticism. Some have questioned his claims about the significance of determinism for our moral responsibility practices, particularly his argument that our commitment to these practices runs too deep, and is too central to our nature, to be disturbed by any discoveries we might make about determinism (G. Strawson [1986] 1993). Suspicion has also been expressed about the related claim that it is impossible, or nearly so, to rid ourselves of the reactive attitudes and that giving up these attitudes would mean abandoning the prospect of holding one another to moral demands (Watson [1987] 2004a: 255–8; Nelkin 2011: 42–5). Some people – Martin Luther King, Jr., and Mahatma Gandhi are often offered as examples – seem to have had some success in giving up at least the *negative* reactive attitudes and to have done so while still confronting wrongdoers with moral demands and attempting to hold them to moral standards. Such exemplars of human conduct do not take up an objective attitude that estranges them from their fellow human beings; in fact, as Gary Watson argues,

> They are often intensely involved in the 'fray' of interpersonal relations…They *stand up* for themselves and others against their oppressors; they *confront* their oppressors with the fact of their misconduct, *urging* and even *demanding* considerations for themselves and others; but they manage, or come much closer than others to managing, to do such things without vindictiveness or malice. ([1987] 2004a: 258)

Another important criticism focuses on Strawson's claim that moral responsibility should be understood in terms of the reactive attitudes and that the practices that feature these attitudes are not assessable by reference to independent facts about moral responsibility. According to Gary Watson's influential interpretation, on Strawson's view, there is no

> independent notion of responsibility that explains the priority of the reactive attitudes. The explanatory priority is the other way around: It is not that we hold people responsible because they *are* responsible; rather, the idea (*our* idea) that we are responsible is to be understood by the practice, which itself is not a matter of holding some propositions to be true, but of expressing our concerns and demands about our treatment of one another. ([1987] 2004a: 222)

John Martin Fischer and Mark Ravizza have argued that, if this picture of moral responsibility were accurate, our moral responsibility practices would be beyond critique in a way that is both implausible and unappealing. If being morally responsible is just a matter of being targeted with reactive attitudes, and there are no independent facts about moral responsibility in virtue of which these attitudes can be assessed, then there is little conceptual room for characterizing instances of praise and blame as unjust, inappropriate, or mistaken. But it seems obvious that we can be mistaken about whether a person is blameworthy for her behavior. We can even imagine that an entire community might have it as part of their practice to praise or blame individuals who are not really open to these responses. For example, as Fischer and Ravizza imagine, there might be groups that wrongly expose the severely mentally handicapped to resentment and punishment for their "bad" behavior (1993: 18).

The problem, as Fischer and Ravizza see it, is that Strawson's approach comes closer to giving us an account of what it is for a person to be *held* morally responsible than it does to giving us a theory of what it is for her *to be* morally responsible (1993: 18). One way of avoiding this problem would be to reject Strawson's approach in favor of a "Ledger view" about moral responsibility. According to Fischer and Ravizza, these views construe "our ascriptions of responsibility as first and foremost judgments concerning an agent's moral value" (ibid.: 17). Jonathan Glover is often interpreted as offering a view of this sort when he describes blame as "a kind of moral accounting, where a person's actions are recorded in an informal balance sheet [i.e., a ledger], with the object of assessing his moral worth" (1970: 64). Similarly, we could say that praise involves the judgment that there is a "credit" on an agent's "ledger of life" or a "luster" on his "record as a person." Michael Zimmerman (1988: 38) collects this last set of phrases from other authors in the course of presenting his own Ledger approach; Haji (1998) is often cited as providing another instance of a Ledger view.

Ledger views avoid Fischer and Ravizza's worry described above because they take assessments of moral responsibility to be prior to, and independent of, the reactive attitudes. However, this feature of Ledger views has led to the criticism that they deliver an account of responsibility – and of moral blame in particular – that is too sterile and emotionally disengaged to do justice to the phenomenon. Gary Watson says that such views make it seem as if, "in blaming," we are "mainly moral clerks, recording moral faults," and clearly takes this to be a mark against these approaches ([1987] 2004a: 226). Similarly, T. M. Scanlon says that such approaches fail to "explain the distinctive weight that moral blame seems to have" and that they are therefore in danger of reducing blame to "a pointless assignment of moral 'grades'" (2008: 127). (It's worth noting that this is similar to one of the objections we saw posed against J. J. C. Smart's consequentialist approach to responsibility. This isn't surprising, since dispassionate moral grading plays a prominent role in Smart's account.)

Of course, Strawson's view, with its focus on the interpersonally engaged reactive attitudes, is largely immune to the concerns expressed by Watson and Scanlon. What we might want, then, is a broadly Strawsonian account of moral responsibility that gives a primary role to the reactive attitudes but that is not subject to Fischer and Ravizza's worry about conflating *being* morally responsible and *being held* morally responsible. In other words, we might want a theory that provides us with an account of when and why a person is properly held morally responsible in the sense of being *appropriately* targeted with reactive attitudes.

In fact, Fischer and Ravizza themselves aim to provide such an account in their influential book *Responsibility and Control* (1998). While the details of their view stray very far from that of Strawson, they still take themselves to be offering a theory of when a person is "*rationally accessible* to the reactive attitudes" and of what it takes to be "'in the ballpark' as a potential candidate for" these attitudes (1998: 7). On their view, a person is a proper target for the reactive attitudes if she exercises "guidance control" over her behavior, and whether a person has this kind of control depends (among other things) on whether she has the right sort of capacity to respond to reasons. Whether an agent has this capacity is determined by the degree to which she would have responded differently to reasons in a range of *counterfactual* scenarios. Since the test for guidance control is in this way counterfactual, it is possible for an agent to exercise guidance control over her behavior – and to be open to the reactive attitudes – even if she could not have acted otherwise in her actual circumstances.

In *Responsibility and the Moral Sentiments* (1996), R. Jay Wallace develops a related, but more explicitly Strawsonian, approach to putting our moral responsibility practices on a firm foundation. Wallace argues that it is appropriate to hold a person to moral demands (and to expose her to negative reactive attitudes when these demands are flouted) only if she possesses certain powers of "reflective self-control" (1996: 17). Once again, possession of these powers of self-control is meant to be compatible with the possibility that the person in question could not have behaved otherwise than she did. More recently, Michael McKenna has offered a distinct account of the appropriateness of the reactive attitudes in *Conversation and Responsibility* (2012). McKenna's basic idea is that wrongdoing, blaming, apologizing, excusing, and so on, are analogous to exchanges in a conversation and ought to be assessed in terms of whether they are intelligible contributions to a moral exchange (for an earlier Strawsonian approach along related lines, see Watson [1987] 2004a). I'll say more about the views of each of these authors in later chapters.

2.4 Attributability and Accountability: Two Faces of Moral Responsibility

So far, I have focused on two quite different approaches to moral responsibility (the forward-looking approach and the reactive attitudes approach; I also briefly described the Ledger view of moral responsibility). In this section, instead of presenting another conceptualization of moral responsibility, I want to introduce Gary Watson's distinction between two "faces" of responsibility. This distinction will help to bring to the surface some of the submerged tensions between the views we have encountered so far.

Watson's distinction arises out of the observation that we can have different interests and aims when it comes to assessing a person's moral responsibility. These differences make it possible to speak of different *kinds* of moral responsibility such that a person might be morally responsible in one sense but not in another: for example, a person might be morally responsible in the *attributability sense* but not in the *accountability sense*. What this would mean is that the person is morally responsible in the sense that her behavior is attributable to her – it really is *her* behavior and it really is morally good or bad behavior – but she is not morally responsible in the further sense of being appropriately held accountable for her behavior. For example, it might not be appropriate to respond to such an agent with hostile attitudes such as resentment even though her conduct was genuinely bad and she acted precisely as she wanted to.

A bit of background is in order before saying more about the distinction between attributability and accountability. I briefly mentioned above P. F. Strawson's suggestion that a person might be exempt from blame if his formative circumstances were especially unfortunate. Strawson doesn't say much to explain or defend this claim, but many people are attracted to the idea that it is unfair to blame a person for bad behavior that is explained largely by deprivations that the person suffered as a child. This is especially true when these deprivations seem to have impaired the person's ability to behave better.

In *Freedom Within Reason* (1990), Susan Wolf criticizes a set of views that have difficulty accommodating the fairly natural perspective just described. According to these approaches – which Wolf calls Real Self views – a person is morally responsible for behavior that springs from her "real self." Roughly speaking, behavior issues from your real self if it is explained by desires that you endorse and that are in conformity with your values. The compulsive stealing of a kleptomaniac, for example, would *not* be attributable to her real self if the urge to steal is one that the kleptomaniac does not endorse and that she regards as alien to who she really is (Wolf 1990: 28, 80). But, according to the Real Self view, if a person *does* endorse the desires that inform her behavior, then the fact that she acquired those desires because of a bad upbringing won't diminish her moral responsibility. Wolf finds this conclusion implausible and, in order to bridge the gap between her own intuitions and those of Real Self theorists, she suggests that the latter must be employing a relatively limited conception of moral blame (ibid.: 39–40).

What the Real Self theorist must suppose, Wolf imagines, is that to blame someone is just to say that he or she is the author of bad actions (in the way that a Ledger theorist might). She agrees that the victim of a deprived childhood can be the author of bad acts, but she argues that the foregoing is at best a superficial form of blame. For Wolf, genuine moral blame is a deeper and more serious affair and something that Real Self approaches apparently have difficulty accommodating, since they cannot acknowledge conditions on blame that seem obvious to her.

Here is where Gary Watson's distinction comes in. In an essay responding to Wolf, Watson acknowledges that some approaches to moral responsibility focus on the nature of a person's behavior and on whether the behavior is really *hers*. He calls these accounts "self-disclosure" views, a designation meant to pick out the same theories as Wolf's "Real Self" views (Watson [1996] 2004b: 261). (Interestingly, Wolf's primary example of a Real Self view is Watson's own earlier work.) Watson's idea is that, when your behavior issues from values that you endorse, it "discloses" something important about where you stand and who you are – it reveals, in other words, something about your "fundamental evaluative orientation" (ibid.: 271).

For Watson, this is not a superficial form of moral responsibility at all: "The self-disclosure view describes a core notion of responsibility that is central to ethical life and ethical appraisal. In virtue of the capacities identified by the self-disclosure view, conduct can be attributable or imputable to an individual as its agent…Attributability in this sense *is* a kind of responsibility" ([1996] 2004b: 263). However, Watson agrees with Wolf that there is more to moral responsibility, and particularly to blameworthiness, than the attribution of bad behavior to an agent. He says, "[h]olding people responsible is not just a matter of the relation of an individual to her behavior" – that is, it goes beyond merely attributing behavior – "it also involves a social setting in which we demand (require) certain conduct from one another and respond adversely to one another's failures to comply with these demands" (ibid.: 262). Similarly, Watson says that "judgments of moral blameworthiness" involve more than an attribution of wrongdoing; they also "involve the idea that agents deserve adverse treatment or 'negative attitudes' in response to their faulty conduct" (ibid.: 266).

So, on Watson's view, when we wonder whether it is reasonable to make moral demands of people or to respond to them with negative attitudes such as resentment, we are no longer concerned exclusively with the question of attributability. We are now concerned with *accountability*, and, according to Watson, the fact that bad behavior is attributable to someone is not enough to make her accountable for that behavior. This is because a person's bad behavior might be attributable to her even though it would be unfair to respond to her with "adverse or unwelcome treatment" (Watson [1996] 2004b: 275). For example, such treatment would be unfair, on Watson's view, if the person to whom bad behavior is attributable lacked the ability to conform her behavior to our moral demands – perhaps because of her unfortunate formative circumstances – and thereby to avoid the sort of unwelcome treatment in question.

Watson illustrates the difference between responsibility-as-attributability and responsibility-as-accountability in the following passage about a hypothetical murderer who was the victim of severe abuse as a child:

> His deliberate and remorseless murders characterize him as malicious and cruel in a sense that no nonreflective being could be. The fact that life gave him a rotten deal, that his squalid circumstances made it overwhelmingly difficult to develop a respect for the standards to which we would hold him accountable, does not impugn these aretaic appraisals [that is, appraisals in terms of virtues and vices; *arête* is a Greek word for "virtue"]. His conduct is attributable to him as an exercise of his "moral capacities." It expresses and constitutes his practical identity, what he stands for, what he has made of his life as he found it.
>
> At the same time, there is an inclination to doubt that such a person can rightly be held accountable, at least fully, that while he might "deserve pity," as [Susan] Wolf says, he "does not deserve blame." This ambivalence mirrors the two faces of responsibility. What gives rise to our "pity" are concerns about fairness. Facts about his formative years give rise to the thought that the individual has already suffered too much and that we too would probably have been morally ruined by such a childhood. What is inhibited by these concerns is accountability blame. ([1996] 2004b: 280–1)

For his influential treatment of a real-life story like this, see Watson ([1987] 2004a). In an important recent paper, David Shoemaker (2011) has expanded on Watson's basic approach, adding a third form of responsibility: responsibility-as-answerability.

2.5 The New Attributionism: Austere Approaches to Blame

Many theorists agree with Watson and Wolf that, if a wrong-doer is seriously impaired in her ability to conform to our moral demands (perhaps, though not necessarily, on account of deprivations that she suffered as a child), it is unfair, or in some other way inappropriate, to respond to her with the robust blaming responses that Watson associates with "accountability blame." This thesis has a lot of intuitive appeal. Consider the murderer described by Watson or think of a person – to use an example of Wolf's – "raised in a society in which false values are too effectively reinforced" (Wolf 1990: 80–1). Given their stultifying upbringings, it might be unreasonable to expect these people to recognize the true moral status of their bad behavior. And if we can't expect people to recognize that their behavior is wrong, how can it be fair to blame them – in the full-blooded sense of account-ability blame – when they don't refrain from that behavior?

As I said, many theorists find the reasoning just sketched appealing, but philosophers pursuing what is sometimes called an *attributionist* approach to moral responsibility have recently called into question aspects of this picture of blame. The label "attributionism" is appropriate insofar as these views tend to regard it as sufficient for blameworthiness that a person's bad behavior is attributable to her in a way that indicates something morally objectionable about her and her orientation toward other people.[1] However, "attributionism" is also a problematic title. For one thing, there are impor-tant differences between these views, and collecting them under a common title tends to obscure this fact. (I introduce below the views of three representative authors, all of whom I somewhat uncomfortably group together as "attributionist"; in §5.4, I note an important difference between two of these authors.)

Another problem is that "attributionism" echoes Watson's terminology in a way that can be misleading. One might imagine, for example, that attributionist views are concerned only with articulating the conditions that apply to the *attribution* of moral faults and not with the appropriateness of the responses involved in holding people *accountable* for their behavior. However, this is not the case (cf. Smith 2012: 576). The recent attributionist approaches I have in mind are concerned with the legitimacy of the responses that Watson associates with accountability blame; it's just that contemporary attributionists believe that wrongdoers can be open to these responses *simply because bad behavior is attributable to them*. So, for attributionists, the satisfaction of relatively weak conditions on blame can open a wrongdoer up to blame in a strong sense. Or, to put it in a slogan (that no doubt elides certain subtleties and distinctions): attributability is enough for accountability. What this means in practice is that attributionists are much less worried than some other philosophers (such as Watson and Wolf) that a wrongdoer's bad upbringing, or her difficulty recognizing the wrongness of an action, makes it unfair to target her with robust blaming responses. Since these factors do nothing to undermine the attribution of a bad action to a wrongdoer, they do nothing – or at least they do very little – to call into question the wrongdoer's blameworthiness and the appropriateness of the moral responses involved in blame.

It might help to avoid confusion with Watson's form of attributionism to refer to the views described in this section as New Attributionism. I'll occasionally use this appellation below and in subsequent chapters; however, it will sometimes be easier to speak simply of "attributionism," and in those cases I should be understood as referring to the view described here.

George Sher

New Attributionist accounts tend to reject the view that people are properly blamed only for what is in their control.

A series of recent books and papers by George Sher provides a good example of this trend.

On Sher's view, blame involves the belief that a person has acted badly, or has a bad character, together with a disposition to feel certain negative emotions (e.g., resentment) toward that person. (Note that this is a mere *disposition*; it is possible, on Sher's account, for blame to occur in the absence of negative emotions.) The belief and disposition are connected by the desire that the person we blame not have acted badly or that she not have a bad character. It is the presence of this desire, and the fact that it is not satisfied, that explains why we are disposed to respond negatively to those who act badly and thereby frustrate our desires. Sher's account, then, looks like this: "To blame someone ... is to have certain affective and behavioral dispositions [i.e., dispositions to respond with negative emotions and treatments], each of which can be traced to the combination of a belief that that person has acted badly or has a bad character and a desire that this not be the case" (2006: 115).

But what makes blame, so understood, appropriate? According to Sher, blame is appropriate when the beliefs and desires that constitute it are themselves appropriate, and this depends on whether a bad action, or a bad character, really is attributable to the agent in question. As Sher puts it, when a "desire–belief pair" of the sort described above "is appropriate to the badness of a person's behavior or character," then the desire–belief pair "is for that very reason deserved by the person himself," as are the blaming dispositions to which the desire–belief pair naturally gives rise (2006: 131).

Now, as Wolf or Watson might point out, it is often out of a person's control whether she has a bad moral character that inclines her toward the morally objectionable behavior that would render appropriate the beliefs and desires involved in blame. But Sher does not regard this as a problem for his view. Of course, it's not appropriate to blame a person who lacked control over his behavior in the sense that it was physically impossible for him to avoid it, but this is because such an action would not reflect badly on the person as a moral agent: it would "not cast a negative shadow on him" (Sher 2006: 58). It's quite a different thing when someone lacks control over her character traits: regardless of how a person acquired a bad trait, possession of such a trait necessarily casts a negative shadow, because "to have a bad trait just *is* to be systematically unresponsive to the corresponding class of moral reasons" (ibid.). Thus, a person's lack of control over her bad traits does nothing to call into question the appropriateness of the belief that she has a bad character and the desire that that not be the case. In other words, "bad people can be blamed simply for being bad" (ibid.: 52).

Of course, being bad – having a bad character – can make it difficult to avoid bad actions, and this might be thought to limit a person's control over her behavior by making it difficult for her to avoid bad actions. This is a potential excusing condition to which accounts such as Watson's and Wolf's are sensitive. But, on Sher's view, it is "no less fair to blame" a person who behaves dishonestly "because he is so corrupt that he sees no point in being honest" than it is "to blame another who sees the point of being honest perfectly well, but who decides ... to give in to a dishonest impulse" (2006: 63). What matters is that both agents have behaved dishonestly; this is enough to license the beliefs and desires involved in blame as well as the blaming responses to which these states give rise.

In his 2009 book *Who Knew?: Responsibility Without Awareness*, Sher expands on his earlier work to argue that people can be morally responsible for behavior over which they lack control in the sense that they are, in some important way, unaware of what they are doing. Sher has in mind cases like those in which a person forgets to fulfill an important obligation or is unaware of the likely bad consequences of her behavior. Such an agent will be open to blame on Sher's account as long as her lack of awareness (i) falls below an applicable standard and (ii) is explicable in terms of internal psychological factors that help to make her the person she is (2009: 88).

Suppose, for example, that in an effort to quiet a crying baby, 23-year-old Scout mixes vodka with the fruit juice she gives to the baby (Sher 2009: 26). She wasn't trying to hurt the baby; it just didn't occur to her that giving vodka to a baby is a dangerous thing to do. Scout's behavior clearly falls below the standard of responsible childcare and, so long as her behavior is explained by traits that belong to her – such as "her impulsiveness...or her tendency not to consider the consequences of what she does" – she will be open to moral blame on Sher's theory (ibid.: 91). If, on the other hand, someone else had secretly put vodka into the baby's juice (and Scout had no way of knowing this), she would not be blameworthy for giving the baby vodka-tainted juice, since this action would not fall below the standard of care that could reasonably be expected of her. Similarly, if Scout had given vodka to the baby only because she had been subjected to some form of mind control, she would not be blameworthy because the psychological factors that explain her behavior would be alien to her – in other words, the behavior would not be attributable *to her* in the right way to support blame.[2]

Angela Smith

In a series of important papers, Angela Smith has developed a perspective that overlaps with Sher's in certain ways. On Smith's view, we can be responsible for – and open to blame on account of – attitudes, desires, and patterns of awareness that we did not choose as long as they reflect, and are sensitive to, our evaluative judgments and commitments – that is, our judgments about the relative value and significance of people and things. Of course, we are not responsible for our unchosen attitudes and patterns of awareness in the sense of having voluntarily brought these things about. Instead, we are responsible for these things in the sense that we can be asked to defend or justify them insofar as they reflect our judgments about what is important. And insofar as our attitudes reflect *objectionable* judgments, they may be a source of the sort of moral offense that reasonably elicits the responses involved in blame.

Smith calls her position the "rational relations" view because, just as there is usually a rational connection or relation between a person's voluntary actions and her judgments about what is important or valuable, there is often a connection between these sorts of judgments and a person's *involuntary* psychological and emotional states. Smith notes that, because of this rational relation, "we often take what a person notices and neglects to have an enormous amount of expressive significance" (2005: 242). For example, a friend might regard it as very telling that I have forgotten her birthday; she might think that my forgetting indicates a lack of concern on my part that makes negative responses, and the expectation of an apology, appropriate (ibid.: 236). Similarly, I may fail to "notice when my music is too loud," or that "my advice is unwelcome," or that "my assistance might be helpful to others," and, even if these failures are involuntary, they may still indicate "that I do not judge your needs and interests to be important, or at least that I do not take them very seriously" (ibid.: 244). And this judgment about you, or this orientation toward you, is something for which I am answerable – something that I can be asked to justify and for which I am potentially open to sanction – just because it belongs to me.

T. M. Scanlon

When Smith emphasizes the importance to us of the evaluative judgments that inform other people's behavior, she is building on an approach to moral responsibility and blame pioneered by T. M. Scanlon. Scanlon's work may be regarded as a paradigm instance of New Attributionist thinking about moral responsibility, and it has influenced a fair amount of the contemporary work that I gather under that heading.

In his book *What We Owe to Each Other*, Scanlon says, "[q]uestions about 'moral responsibility' are most often questions about whether some action can be attributed to an agent in the way that is required ... for it to be a basis for moral appraisal" of that agent (1998: 248). A potential worry about this approach – a worry that we've considered in different forms above – is that it threatens to reduce moral blame to something like J. J. C. Smart's "dispraise." In other words, perhaps Scanlon's view implausibly presents blame as merely a negative evaluation of a person's attributes or – even worse – "a pointless assignment of moral 'grades,'" as we saw Scanlon put it in his criticism of Ledger views. (See Wallace 1996: 80–1 and Watson 2002: 240 for the worry that Scanlon's view identifies blame with mere negative appraisal.)

Scanlon argues that his view avoids this worry in a couple of ways, both of which involve narrowing the focus of blame (1998: 275–7, 287). First, on Scanlon's view, the criticism involved in moral blame focuses on instances in which a person has displayed morally faulty self-governance – that is, cases in which an agent has "governed him- or herself in a manner that cannot be justified in the way morality requires" (ibid.: 272). Thus a negative evaluation of a person's height would not count as an instance of moral blame because a person's height is not usually the result of faulty self-governance. To use Scanlon's terminology, a person's height (or her eye color) is not "judgment-sensitive": it is not responsive to an agent's judgments about what reasons she has and therefore it is not something that the agent can be asked to defend, to apologize for, or to modify in the way that is characteristic of holding a person morally responsible. On the other hand, states such as "fear, anger, admiration, [and] respect" *are* judgment-sensitive (ibid.: 20): they respond to and reflect our judgments about what we have reason to do and to feel. Thus, when these states are objectionable, they (and the actions that indicate their presence) can often be an appropriate basis for blame.

Of course, not all faulty judgment-sensitive states, and the actions associated with them, are appropriate candidates for moral blame. For example, when a person makes a bad move in a game of chess, this presumably reflects a judgment she made about how to move her pieces, and a poor chess move is an apt candidate for a certain kind of criticism. However, poor self-governance in the context of chess does not usually amount to a *moral* failure, so the associated criticism does not amount to moral blame. Moral blame targets instances of self-governance that "have a particular kind of [moral] significance for that agent's relations with other people," and the way a person plays chess usually does not have this sort of significance (Scanlon 1998: 276).

Scanlon fleshes out the connection between blame and our relationships with other people in his book *Moral Dimensions* (2008). There, he says:

> to claim that a person is *blameworthy* for an action is to claim
> that the action shows something about the agent's attitudes

toward others that impairs the relations that others can have with him or her. To *blame* a person is to judge him or her to be blameworthy and to take your relationship with him or her to be modified in a way that this judgment of impaired relations holds to be appropriate. (2008: 128–9)

Of course, what often impairs a person's relationships with others is just that she has governed herself in a way that betrays an objectionable evaluative orientation toward these others: she has governed herself "in a way that shows a lack of concern with the justifiability of his or her actions, or an indifference to considerations that justifiable standards of conduct require one to attend to" (ibid.: 141).

An important Strawsonian element in Scanlon's approach to moral responsibility should be evident. Whereas Strawson emphasizes the significance of the quality of a person's will for our relationships with her, Scanlon emphasizes the significance of the quality of an agent's *judgments*. Despite this difference in emphasis, it is plausible, I think, to characterize both approaches as drawing attention to our concern for how other people – particularly *some* other people – are oriented toward us and whether they take our needs and interests into account in the ways that we believe they should. This concern is naturally linked to the various expectations that structure our interpersonal relations, and on Strawson's view, as well as on Scanlon's, the failure to live up to these expectations is a central instance of moral blameworthiness.

An important difference between Strawson and Scanlon has to do with the form that "blaming responses" can take. Strawson focuses in this context on negative emotional responses such as indignation and resentment. For Scanlon, however, you engage in blame when you revise or modify your relationship with a person in a way that your judgment of blameworthiness holds to be appropriate. The modifications to our relationships that constitute instances of blame might include emotional responses such as resentment, but they don't have to: we might simply resolve not to trust a former confidant any longer or to cease valuing time spent with a former friend.

In dispensing with the necessity (though not the permissibility) of attitudes such as resentment, Scanlon's view resembles Sher's (for objections to this somewhat sanitized approach to blame, see Wallace 1996: 76–7; Wallace 2013; and McGeer 2013). Scanlon's view also resembles Sher's (and Smith's) insofar as he allows that a person can be morally responsible for things that are not under his direct volitional control (1998: 277ff.). Note, for example, that judgment-sensitive attitudes such as anger, fear, and admiration are not necessarily under our voluntary control, but this doesn't alter the interpersonal significance of these attitudes or their attributability to the agent in question.

More generally, and again like Sher, Scanlon is relatively unconcerned with *how* a person came to have the attitudes he has and how he came to be the sort of self-governor he is. Perhaps a person who governs himself badly does so because of forces beyond his control that negatively affected his moral development as a child, but, if these facts about the agent's history do nothing to call into question the attributability of objectionable judgments to the agent, they do nothing to call into question his blameworthiness (Scanlon 1998: 284–5). On Scanlon's approach, a judgment of moral responsibility interprets an agent's actions and attitudes as indicating faulty self-governance, and, in order for this judgment to be appropriate, "we need *not* also conclude that [the agent] is responsible for becoming the person he now is" (ibid.: 284, emphasis added).

Gary Watson describes Scanlon's account of moral responsibility as "austere" (2002: 240). In part, he means that Scanlon's view is "detached" and "too thin" because it is too narrowly focused on moral appraisals and not on the fittingness of "certain kinds of treatment in view of those appraisals" (ibid.). As I indicated in the introduction to this section, the merit of this criticism is, in my view, questionable, but Scanlon's view is certainly *austere* in the sense that it gets by with little in the way of necessary conditions on moral responsibility (and the context of Watson's discussion suggests that this is part of what he had in mind in choosing that expression). Indeed, Scanlon doesn't even require that a blameworthy agent must be able to respond appropriately to moral reasons (1998: 287–9; 2008: 233 n.54); all that's required is that a morally objectionable judgment or attitude is attributable to the agent. Thus, on Scanlon's view, even a psychopath will turn out to be blameworthy if he is able to express through his behavior the kinds of interpersonally significant attitudes and judgments to which blame responds. (I discuss the status of psychopaths in detail in chapter 4.)

In the interests of full disclosure I should note that I find the New Attributionist perspective – particularly as it is developed by Smith and Scanlon – very appealing, and I have defended aspects of it in various places. In upcoming chapters I'll often suggest that this view can be usefully applied in various ways to resolve puzzles about moral responsibility; however, I'll also point out places where New Attributionism may be thought to fall short.

2.6   Judging Blameworthy versus Blaming

I turn now to an important distinction (related to one noted in §2.3) that is associated with attributionists such as Scanlon and Smith, though one need not accept their views in order to find the distinction helpful.

It seems that we can, and perhaps that we should, distinguish between the judgment that a person is blameworthy and actually blaming her. For Scanlon, to judge that a person is morally blameworthy is to take her actions or attitudes to indicate that she has governed herself in a way that is morally faulty and that impairs our relationship with her. However, on Scanlon's view, even when such a judgment is accurate, it is a separate question whether we should *express* the moral criticism that is implicit in a judgment of blameworthiness (1998: 269, 285, 289–90; 2008: 175–9, 187–8, 197–8). A number of considerations might count against expressing moral criticism even when that criticism is, considered on its own, apt. Perhaps a particular piece of moral criticism applies just as well to me as to the person that I propose to blame, so it would be hypocritical of me to offer the criticism; or perhaps the criticism would be, in one way or another, pointless, cruel, or excessive. All these considerations might give me good reason to refrain from actively expressing blame even when the agent in question is blameworthy. We can, of course, disagree about whether one ought to refrain from hypocritical blame (Bell 2013) or about whether a particular expression of criticism would count as cruel or excessive, but Scanlon's general point is clear enough: a judgment of blame-worthiness is different from – and answers to different constraints than – the expression of this judgment.

Angela Smith brings this general point into sharper focus in her essay "On Being Responsible and Holding Responsible," where she argues that "our intuitions about whether and when it would be fair to react negatively to another are sensitive to a host of considerations that appear to have little or nothing to do with an agent's responsibility or culpability" (2007: 466). If Smith is right, then we should distinguish between these two things – an agent's responsibility and our reactions toward the agent – and we should be wary of moving too quickly from the fact that it would be inappropriate actively to blame a person to the conclusion that she is not blameworthy (ibid.: 467). In fact, it may be inappropriate actively to blame a person for reasons that do nothing to call into question her moral responsibility. This point can also be put the other way around: "it does not follow directly from the judgment that a person is responsible and culpable, that it would be appropriate to adopt or express blaming attitudes" (ibid.).

Smith offers the following example:

> If a good friend of mine is under a lot of stress, for example, I may not "hold" her responsible, in the sense of actively blaming her, for some insensitive comments she makes to me. I can judge both that she *is* responsible for her comments, and that she *is* open to legitimate moral criticism for them (because they are hurtful). But given the circumstances, I may decide that it would be uncharitable for me to take up attitudes of anger and resentment, or to explicitly reproach her in any way. (2007: 470)

We might say that Smith's friend fulfills the *responsibility condition* on being open to active blame even though other factors speak against blaming her. Considerations that speak against expressions of blame include the possibility that it is, in one way or another, not "our place" to blame a particular person (ibid.: 478), or that the fault in question is too minor to warrant such an expression (ibid.: 480), or even that the blameworthy agent has already reproached herself to an extent that makes additional expressions of blame inappropriate (ibid.: 482).

In some ways, Smith's distinction is similar to Watson's contrast between attributability blame and accountability blame: as we saw, on Watson's account, an agent may be blameworthy in one sense, but not in the sense that licenses certain *expressions* of blame. There is, however, a crucial difference between Smith's distinction and Watson's. On Smith's view, an agent might meet all the responsibility conditions that apply to blame and yet attitudes such as resentment might be inappropriate for other reasons. However, in the examples to which Watson appeals, when an agent is presented as not being open to blaming responses, this is meant to be because he has not fulfilled important responsibility-relevant conditions.

As I noted in chapter 1, words such as "blame" and "responsibility" are used in many different ways, and this diversity can generate confusion. Keeping the difference between judgments of blameworthiness and actual blaming responses in mind (as well as the different standards that might apply to these two things) can help us avoid some of this confusion.

2.7 Conclusion

As we saw at the end of chapter 1, at the heart of Harry Frankfurt's compatibilism about moral responsibility is the proposal that an agent might act for her own reasons even when she cannot perform a different action than the one she performs. In this chapter, we've seen *why* it should matter, when it comes to judging moral responsibility, that a person has guided her behavior in light of her judgments about what reasons she has for acting. It matters because, when a person's judgments about reasons inform her behavior, the behavior can tell us something about how she evaluates the needs and interests of other people, and our practices of praise and blame are very sensitive to our perceptions of these evaluations. (It's worth noting that incompatibilists can embrace elements of the foregoing perspective: acknowledging the importance, on the grounds just given, of acting for one's own reasons does not by itself commit one to compatibilism.)

One issue that has come up at several points in this chapter is the contrast between accounts that interpret blame primarily as a form of moral assessment and accounts that focus on the responses – often the emotional responses – involved in blame. In particular, we've seen that views of the former sort are sometimes criticized for being sterile and incomplete insofar as they fail to (fully) acknowledge the personally engaged, reactive side of blame.

No doubt this description is accurate in some cases. J. J. C. Smart, for example, thinks of blame mainly as moral grading, with any sanctioning responses ideally resulting from an impartial calculation of their likely results. In other cases, however, the criticism in question is less apt. It's true, for example, that New Attributionists such as T. M. Scanlon view blame as fundamentally having to do with the attribution of moral faults to agents, but this doesn't mean that these accounts are unconcerned with justifying the personally engaged and responsive aspects of "holding responsible." What separates these attributionist views from other accounts is not a lack of interest in the engaged and responsive elements of moral responsibility but, rather, the contention that satisfaction of the attribution conditions on responsibility is what licenses the further elements. In subsequent chapters we will encounter a number of additional proposed conditions on moral responsibility (which attributionists tend to reject), conditions having to do with an agent's personal history, psychological powers, and moral knowledge.

2.8   Further Reading

All the anthologies and monographs mentioned at the end of the last chapter are also relevant to several of the topics in this chapter. There are, in addition, a number of collections of essays with a more than usual focus on the topics presented here (as opposed to the issues about free will and determinism discussed in the last chapter): these include Coates and Tognazzini (2013b) and McKenna and Russell (2008), the latter of which collects essays on P. F. Strawson's "Freedom and Resentment." Additionally, several of the essays in the edited volume by Wallace, Kumar, and Freeman (2011) focus on T. M. Scanlon's account of moral responsibility. The recently inaugurated *Oxford Studies in Agency and Responsibility* will also certainly be of value: two volumes are already in print; the second, edited by David Shoemaker and Neal Tognazzini, again focuses on "Freedom and Resentment." The *Stanford Encyclopedia of Philosophy* should also be consulted, particularly Eshleman's entry "Moral Responsibility" (2014) and Tognazzini and Coates's "Blame" (2014).

3

History, Luck, and Skepticism

In this chapter we will consider a number of related issues having to do with the processes by which people acquire their individual characters, values, and desires. We will ask, for example, about the degree of control people need to exercise over these processes in order to be morally responsible for their behavior. An important skeptical worry arises in this domain because of the possibility that the features of our selves that lead us to act as we do are ultimately explained by factors over which we have no control.

To set the stage, consider this famous passage from the beginning of Karl Marx's *Eighteenth Brumaire of Louis Napoleon*: "Men make their own history, but they do not make it just as they please; they do not make it under circumstances chosen by themselves, but under circumstances directly found, given and transmitted from the past" ([1852] 1972: 437). It's evident that we do not create the world in which we find ourselves and in which we perform our actions. We may make contributions to the world, but these are contributions to something that already exists, and the pre-existing circumstances in which we make our choices necessarily limit the kinds of contributions that we can make. But if the world in which we find ourselves – and for which we are therefore not responsible – structures the kinds of changes to the world that we can make, does this undermine our responsibility for making these changes? The issue becomes even more pressing when we recognize that not only are we not responsible for the world in which we find ourselves, we are not responsible for the tools – our innate strengths and weaknesses, our initial access to resources, and so on – that we use to shape it.

3.1　Moral Luck

We'll start with the phenomenon of "moral luck" and Thomas Nagel's famous 1976 essay of the same name. Part of Nagel's aim is to undermine a perspective that's initially very appealing: namely, the view "that people cannot be morally assessed for what is not their fault, or for what is due to factors beyond their control" ([1976] 1979: 25). There are many cases that appear to support this claim. As we saw in earlier chapters, if a person's behavior is out of her control in the sense that it is involuntary (for example, the product of a muscle spasm or of coercion), she is likely excused from moral judgment even if the consequences of her behavior are quite bad.

However, and as Nagel notes, our ordinary practices of moral assessment often seem to involve holding people morally responsible for actions even when the results of the action, or the factors that contributed to the agent's performance of the action, are outside the agent's control. From an agent's perspective, the elements of an action that are out of her control are a matter of luck. Thus, on Nagel's view, an accurate account of moral responsibility must tolerate a certain amount of *moral luck*, which is what occurs when "a significant aspect of what someone does depends on factors beyond his control, yet we continue to treat him in that respect as an object of moral judgment" ([1976] 1979: 26).

Think, for example, of the difference between *murder* and *attempted murder*. Isn't a murderer more worthy of condemnation than a person who merely, and unsuccessfully, attempts to commit murder? But it's quite possible that all that kept an attempt at murder from being successful was a bit of luck; such an attempt might fail even though the attempter did everything in his power to achieve his aim.

Perhaps an assassin's rifle jammed when he tried to fire it even though he took special care to clean his weapon the night before in order to prevent just such an occurrence.

Is the fact that a would-be assassin's rifle jammed relevant to our moral assessment of him? This may seem odd, but, again, it is natural to say that there's a big moral difference between being guilty of murder and being guilty of attempted murder, and what makes this a case of attempted murder is the fact that the assassin's rifle jammed. And if the fact that the rifle jammed *is* relevant to our moral assessment, we must admit that luck is relevant to moral assessment, since, from the assassin's perspective, it was merely a matter of luck that his rifle jammed. The assassin might think of it as bad luck since it frustrated his effort to achieve a goal, but we might say that he had good moral luck because his moral record is better than it would have been if he had killed someone.

A similar analysis can be given in cases of unintentional behavior. Suppose that you accidently drive through a red light because you're talking on your cell phone. Luckily for you, there was no pedestrian in the intersection that you carelessly drove through; if there had been, however, you surely would have hit him. Many people have the sense that, if you had hit a pedestrian, you would be worthy of a degree of blame of which you are not worthy since there actually was no pedestrian in the intersection. Of course, in the case in which no pedestrian is present, we may still think that you are blameworthy, since talking on your cell phone while driving is careless (or even reckless), but many people would regard you as less blameworthy than if you had actually run someone over.

Why should this be so? After all, the version of the story in which you hit a pedestrian and the version in which you don't may be identical as far as your contribution is concerned. That is, you could have been driving in an identically careless fashion, in identical cars, down identical streets (except for the presence of the pedestrian) in both versions of the story. But, if this is so, it seems that the difference in your blameworthiness in the two versions of the story depends on something that is out of your control: the fact that a pedestrian was, or was not, in your path. On the one hand, this may seem inappropriate – shouldn't our assessment of you depend just on the contributions that *you* make to your actions? On the other hand, it is hard to resist the conclusion that a careless driver who hits a pedestrian has done something worse and has a worse moral record than a careless driver who does not (even if the second driver is just as careless as the first).

The preceding cases involve luck in what happens *after* an agent has made her contribution to a certain outcome. Something similar happens in what Nagel describes as "decisions under uncertainty" ([1976] 1979: 29). Sometimes a person must make an important choice under conditions that make it very difficult for her to see how things will turn out, but how things turn out may significantly affect how we assess the agent for the choice she made. Consider one of Nagel's examples. The leaders of the American Revolution (George Washington, Thomas Jefferson, etc.) are revered in the United States as gifted military and political leaders, but if things had turned out differently – if their revolt had been "a bloody failure resulting in greater repression" (ibid.: 30) – they might be regarded today as foolhardy and naïve, even though nothing else changed about their choices or the circumstances under which they made them. (It is phenomena of this general sort that Bernard Williams [1976] 1981 originally dubbed "moral luck" in his paper by that name; Nagel's paper was originally a response to Williams.)

Moral luck can also play a role in explaining why an agent made the choices she did (rather than just explaining why the choices she made gave rise to certain consequences). For instance, a person might be lucky or unlucky in the moral circumstances in which she finds herself and the moral tests that she faces. We can think of the "ordinary citizens of Nazi Germany" who chose to support or to oppose the Nazi regime as having faced a test, and very many of them failed that test (Nagel [1976] 1979: 34). But, before we condemn the ordinary German, we would do well to remember that most of us have had the good fortune never to have faced such a test, so we never ran the risk of having our moral records tarnished in this way. The worry, then, is not just that the Germans had bad moral luck in finding themselves in the circumstances they did, but also that *we* had good luck in not finding ourselves in similar circumstances. Once again we seem to be, as Nagel puts it, "morally at the mercy of fate" and, he adds, "it may seem irrational upon reflection, but our ordinary moral attitudes would be unrecognizable without it" (ibid.).

Of course, one might say that the citizens of Nazi Germany behaved as they did not just because of their circumstances but also because of their individual moral constitutions and the way their moral characters interacted with their circumstances. But here again we encounter a form of luck: constitutive moral luck. That is, luck in how a person is constituted – luck in having the inclinations, capacities, and temperament that one happens to have. Though Nagel says comparatively little about it, this form of moral luck is especially important since, as we'll see, it plays a prominent role in skepticism about moral responsibility.

An Initial Response to the Problem of Moral Luck

How should we respond to the problem presented by moral luck? We might try to banish luck from our moral practices and to give an account of responsibility that explicitly rules it out. We could say, for example, that people are morally responsible only for what is in their control and for what they themselves contribute to their actions. If we take this approach, then we would say that the blameworthiness of a careless driver does not depend on whether there happened to be a pedestrian in his path; his blameworthiness would depend only on the fact that he was careless. And if there were *two* careless drivers, but only one of them had the misfortune of finding a pedestrian in his path, we would regard them as equivalently blameworthy if they were equivalently careless. (It would be a further question whether we ought to treat the driver who did not hit a pedestrian as if he had, or whether we should do things the other way around.)

Unfortunately, the approach just described doesn't do away with moral luck entirely. After all, the very carelessness involved in the above examples may have been the product of moral luck, since careless drivers don't necessarily *choose* to drive carelessly. Suppose, for example, that an instance of careless driving arises from a lapse in the driver's attention

– perhaps she slipped into a daydream or she was thinking about the job interview to which she was driving. Such a lapse in attention is typically something that happens to us, not something we intentionally bring about, and being subject to such a lapse might be just as much an instance of bad moral luck as encountering a pedestrian on the crosswalk.

In response, we could switch our focus to cases of voluntary behavior, but it's not clear that things will go much better in this context. Consider again the would-be assassin described earlier, but suppose that his rifle does not jam and that he ends up murdering someone. This means that the assassin was not subject to one form of moral luck (since he didn't have the good moral luck of his rifle jamming) but we might still ask *why* he voluntarily chose to commit murder. Why did committing murder seem to this particular agent, at that particular time, to be the thing to do? The force of this worry – essentially a worry about constitutive moral luck – becomes apparent when we consider the possibility that the assassin's choice may in the end be explained by factors over which he had little control: facts about his upbringing, his genetics, and so on. We'll return to this worry at several points below.

Luck and Skepticism about Moral Responsibility

It's probably starting to become clear why thinking about moral luck leads some people to skepticism about moral responsibility. Here's the problem: once we take into account all the forms of moral luck – the sorts that contribute to an agent making the choices she makes together with the sorts of luck that take over after an agent has made her choice – there doesn't seem to be much left over that an agent can be responsible for. As Nagel puts it,

> The area of genuine agency, and therefore of legitimate moral judgment, seems to shrink under this scrutiny to an extension-less point. Everything seems to result from the combined influence of factors, antecedent and posterior to action, that are not within the agent's control. Since he cannot be responsible for them, he cannot be responsible for their results ... ([1976] 1979: 35)

More generally, recognizing the exhaustive role that antecedent and posterior factors play in explaining behavior can encourage us to take up an objective, external perspective on all exercises of agency, including our own. When we consider behavior from this objective perspective, it can appear to be simply part of the order of events – things that *happen* rather than things that are *done*. From this vantage point, all moral assessment is called into question because "the self which acts and is the object of moral judgment is threatened with dissolution by the absorption of its acts and impulses into the class of events" (ibid.: 36).[3] Nagel, however, does not seem to fully embrace a skeptical conclusion. He recognizes that the objective perspective is one that we can occupy, but he doesn't take this fact to undermine our moral practices. Instead, our practices simply take this fact into account, even if it sits uncomfortably with some of our pre-reflective intuitions about moral responsibility. But others have been led to full-blown skepticism by reflecting on the extent of moral luck and the way our actions are explained by factors beyond our control. The most thorough skeptical account of moral luck along these lines is Neil Levy's book *Hard Luck* (2011b).

Levy defends a position that he calls the "hard luck view." According to this view, "agents are not morally responsible for their actions because luck ensures that there are no desert-entailing differences between moral agents" (2011b: 10). In other words, because of the way luck contributes to everyone's behavior, people don't deserve to be treated differently – to be blamed, for example – simply on account of their moral shortcomings. Levy allows that there might be consequentialist considerations that count in favor of treating people differently, but he believes that the presence of moral luck precludes the justification of differential treatment purely on grounds of moral desert.

In chapter 2, we encountered one set of views that has a ready approach for avoiding skepticism based on concerns about (some forms of) moral luck. I referred to these views as New Attributionist theories of moral responsibility; in *Hard Luck*, Levy calls them quality of will theories (2011b: 158 n.2). On this sort of approach, what makes a person blameworthy is simply that an objectionable action or attitude is attributable to her in a way that opens her up to negative moral assessment. But the fact that a person does not entirely control the way she is – that she is subject to constitutive moral luck, in other words – does not entail that her behavior is not attributable to her or that it is not objectionable. For example, the fact that a person had a bad upbringing, and that this explains her current tendency to treat other people with contempt or disregard, changes neither the fact that she treats other people this way nor the moral significance of this treatment. Given this, the attributionist is likely to claim that a bad upbringing does little to make a wrongdoer a less apt candidate for blame.

On the other hand, when we see how a person's objectionable orientation toward others results from her upbringing, perhaps this really ought to change our attitudes toward this person. Perhaps we should reconsider the moral significance of the person's behavior or the attributability of the behavior to her. Perhaps we should take a more objective perspective on the behavior, coming to see it as more like a destructive (but impersonal) natural phenomenon than a full-blooded exercise of moral agency. At any rate, by some route or another, we may think that the person who is subject to bad constitutive luck is not a proper candidate for blaming responses and that it is therefore unfair to impose the burden of blame on her. According to Levy, attributionism's willingness to blame a wrongdoer who was a victim of bad constitutive luck involves subjecting her to "a double dose of unfairness": "We blame her, *now*" because of the way she is, but the way she is results from how "she was treated unfairly in the *past*...Punishing now is heaping unfairness on unfairness" (2011b: 196).

It's also worth noting in this context that it is quite unclear that attributionism can deal effectively with moral luck *in outcomes*. T. M. Scanlon, a prominent attributionist, has argued that, if an initial fault – a bit of carelessness, say – unluckily leads to outsized bad consequences, this "increases the significance of that [initial] fault for those who have been affected by it...the causal outcome...multiplies the significance of" the fault (2008: 150). Scanlon argues that the increased significance of the initial fault makes increased blame appropriate. There's something natural about this view, and it's obvious that bad luck in outcomes can increase the significance of an original act *in some sense*. However, as we saw in the last chapter, what makes an action or outcome significant (in a blame-grounding way) for Scanlon is that it is related to an objectionable judgment. But bad luck in outcomes can't make the judgments to which these outcomes are traced any more objectionable than they originally were, so it's hard to see how such luck can increase the kind of moral significance that's relevant for blame.

The Ubiquity of Moral Luck

In discussions of constitutive moral luck, the focus tends to fall on cases of people with bad upbringings who do bad things, but it's important to remember that moral luck is meant to be an entirely general phenomenon. Every wrongdoer has bad moral luck in his history; otherwise, he wouldn't be inclined toward wrongdoing. This means that an upbringing that might appear rather fortunate will count as bad moral luck if it leads a person to acquire bad moral values.

Consider the recent case of a Texas juvenile named Ethan. In 2013, at the age of sixteen, Ethan killed four pedestrians and injured two others while driving drunk in a truck he had "borrowed" from his father. Ethan pled guilty to four counts of "intoxication manslaughter" (among other things), but he received a notably lenient sentence: several years of probation plus a stay at an expensive California treatment facility, for which his parents paid. Ethan's light sentence was due in part to his lawyers' successful use of an "affluenza" defense. Ethan was the son of a wealthy businessman, and his team of lawyers argued that since the boy was raised in an environment of wealth and privilege he had not learned to take seriously the consequences of his past bad behavior, so he should not be held fully responsible for his present bad behavior. Of course, Ethan's light sentence would seem to exacerbate the problem to which his lawyers pointed in order to achieve the sentence. As the prosecutor in the case said after the trial: "There can be no doubt that [Ethan] will be in another courthouse one day blaming the lenient treatment he received here" (Muskal 2013).

Ethan's case illustrates several forms of luck. He had the sort of wealth and privilege that many would envy, and he was fortunate that his parents could afford to spend hundreds of thousands of dollars on lawyers and treatment, but, if Ethan's lawyers are correct, his lucky material circumstances were also an instance of bad moral luck. So bad constitutive luck can arise in surprising ways, and the same is presumably true of good moral luck. In fact, whatever kind of upbringing you had is (part of) your moral luck, but whether that luck was good or bad won't always be obvious from the facts of your upbringing. Whatever your upbringing was like, it was good moral luck insofar as it leads you to good behavior and it was bad moral luck insofar as it leads to bad behavior.

3.2   Ultimate Responsibility

In this section, I'll describe the role that reference to "ultimate responsibility" plays in debates about moral responsibility. I'll begin with a skeptical argument based on the idea (related to themes raised in the last section) that it is impossible for a person to be ultimately morally responsible for her actions. Next, I'll move to a libertarian incompatibilist approach to moral responsibility that claims that a form of ultimate moral responsibility is indeed possible.

The "Basic Argument" for Non-Responsibility

In "The Impossibility of Moral Responsibility," Galen Strawson (P. F. Strawson's son) presents several versions of what he calls the Basic Argument, which he says "appears to prove that we cannot be truly or ultimately morally responsible for our actions" ([1994] 2003: 212). The argument is "basic" both in the sense that it is relatively uncomplicated and because it develops a set of concerns that seem to underlie other arguments for skepticism about moral responsibility. Strawson's argument is, for example, closely related to skeptical worries raised by moral luck, particularly by constitutive moral luck.

One version of the Basic Argument begins by noting that you do what you do because of the way you are, particularly the way you are in "certain crucial mental respects" (Strawson [1994] 2003: 219). To simplify things (and following Strawson), let's refer to the mental states that inform a person's behavior – her inclinations, dispositions, and so on – as that person's "nature." Strawson's argument is that, to be truly responsible for your actions, you must be responsible for the nature that leads you to act as you do. But, to be responsible for your nature, that nature must be something that you chose in a way that makes you responsible for it. However, you would be responsible for that choice – the choice of your nature – only if it issued from a pre-existing nature of yours for which you are also responsible. (If your choice of a nature did *not* issue from a pre-existing nature of yours for which you are responsible, how could it count as *your* choice and how could such a choice confer responsibility?) But, to be responsible for your pre-existing nature, you must have chosen it in a way that makes you responsible for it, and so the same problem arises for the pre-existing nature: in order to be responsible for it, and the choices that flow from it, you must have chosen it in light of a nature for which you were already responsible. At each level this problem recurs. It seems, then, that we cannot be responsible for our own natures because a person cannot be the ultimate cause of her own nature and, since we cannot be responsible for our natures, we cannot be truly responsible for the actions we perform in light of our natures.

Suppose that we agree with Strawson that a person cannot create his own nature or be his own cause – that he cannot be *causa sui*, to use the Latin expression. We might still think that we can shape our given natures in various ways and that this grounds a degree of responsibility for our subsequent behavior. This line of thought has a venerable history going all the way back to Aristotle's *Nicomachean Ethics*. As Aristotle notes, a person might fail to consider the likely consequences of his actions because inattention is a feature of his character; he is simply "the sort of person who is inattentive" (1999: 38 [1114a]). However, Aristotle thinks that such a person is still responsible for the consequences of his behavior because "he is himself responsible for becoming this sort of person, because he has lived carelessly. Similarly, an individual is responsible for being unjust, because he has cheated, and for being intemperate, because he has passed his time in drinking and the like" (ibid.). So, on Aristotle' account, the drunkard or the constitutionally inattentive person is open to blame because he made bad choices that led him to acquire bad traits. Likewise, a person might develop a virtue such as courage by choosing to spend time with, and to emulate, people who possess this virtue. For a related contemporary perspective, see Michele Moody-Adams (1990).

Perhaps it is true, as Aristotle suggests, that we can mold our characters in certain ways even if we cannot be the original authors of our own natures. However, this won't persuade a skeptic like Galen Strawson. After all, even if a drunkard's past choices have shaped his character, those past choices must themselves have resulted from facts about how he was inclined to govern himself, and the fact that he was inclined in one way, and not in another, is presumably something for which the drunkard is not ultimately responsible. Similarly, even if I take steps to develop a certain virtue, it is still the case that the choice to improve my character will have resulted from dispositions that I did not choose (and that I was morally lucky to have). In sum, it seems unavoidable that at some point we simply find ourselves as we are: even if we can make choices about the sort of person we want to be, those choices are made from the perspective of the person that we already are.

So, for a skeptic like Strawson, genuine moral responsibility requires being the ultimate or fundamental source of our own behavior, but, since we cannot be the ultimate source of our own behavior, we cannot meet the conditions on genuine moral responsibility. We might think, however, that Strawson has set the standard for moral responsibility too high. For example, John Martin Fischer characterizes Strawson as arguing that moral responsibility requires "total control" of our behavior – in other words, control over all the causal inputs of our behavior, making us the ultimate and sole source of that behavior (2006c: 116). But not only is this standard impossible to achieve, it is also deeply counter-intuitive. Think about all the occurrences and non-occurrences that contribute to your being the way you are and behaving as you do. This list would include not just statements about your temperament and inclinations but also a vast number of cooperating facts: the fact, for example, that a meteorite didn't destroy the town in which you were raised. "Does it not seem highly counter-intuitive," Fischer asks,

> to suppose that I am not a morally responsible agent in virtue of the fact that I had no control over whether the earth was hit by a meteorite or the sun flickered out when I was young…?How could my moral responsibility hinge on whether or not I can prevent the sun from rising or flickering out? We do not have "ultimate responsibility," but it would seem much more plausible to suppose…that such responsibility is not required for genuine, legitimate moral responsibility than to conclude that we are thereby rendered incapable of being held morally responsible. (Ibid.: 113–14)

Strawson is not without response here. In *Hard Luck*, Neil Levy (responding directly to Fischer) argues that our lack of control over the sources of our own agency threatens moral responsibility not because it is incompatible with total control but because it is incompatible with "relevant control": the kind of control that is relevant to questions about moral responsibility (2011b: 5). So Levy can agree with Fischer that control over whether the earth was hit by a meteorite is not relevant to moral responsibility; he simply insists that there are other things over which we would need to have control (our moral characters might be an example) in order to be morally responsible, and that we do not have control over these things.

A different way of arguing against Galen Strawson's skepticism would be simply to deny the relevance of history to moral responsibility. For example, one might hold a consequentialist theory of moral responsibility of the sort considered at the beginning of chapter 2. In this case, we would regard the practices associated with responsibility as simply aiming at fewer instances of socially undesirable behavior. If one adopts such a view then concerns about ultimate responsibility will get little traction, since the consequences of holding an agent responsible do not depend on whether she played a role in coming to be the sort of person that she is. However, as we also saw in chapter 2, consequentialist approaches to moral responsibility tend to be revisionary in a way that many theorists hope to avoid.

As we saw at the end of our discussion of moral luck, the relevance of history for moral responsibility also tends to be denied by New Attributionist approaches. Again, these views hold that judgments of moral responsibility are fundamentally judgments about what can be attributed to a person for the purposes of moral assessment, and, in order to form this sort of judgment, we need not take into account how a person came to be the way that he is. From this perspective, we might worry that Strawson is running together causal and moral conceptions of responsibility. Strawson identifies true moral responsibility with ultimate responsibility, but the latter seems to be primarily a causal notion: a person is ultimately responsible for some outcome only if she is the causal source of that outcome. But why should we grant that this is what true moral responsibility or true blameworthiness comes to? Perhaps what it is to be open to moral blame is just for objectionable behavior to be attributable to you as an exercise, or as a reflection, of your power of guiding your behavior as you see fit.

Of course, someone defending Strawson's view will respond that, given the universal lack of ultimate responsibility, it is never the case that a person's moral faults are attributable to her in a way that could justify the sanctions involved in moral blame. A skeptic who takes this line might argue that what genuine, full-blooded blameworthiness requires is a kind of *ultimate attributability* of moral faults to an agent – a deep ownership of one's flaws – and that this would require an impossible form of self-creation.

Indeterminism and Self-Forming Actions

Robert Kane argues that we can be ultimately responsible for our actions because we can engage in genuinely self-forming activity. For Kane, self-formation does not require an impossible act of self-creation; it simply requires precisely placed instances of indeterminism. I draw mostly on Kane (2007) below, but he develops his view in other places as well, most notably in his book *The Significance of Free Will* (1996).

According to Kane, "*To be ultimately responsible for an action, an agent must be responsible for anything that is a sufficient cause or motive for the action's occurring*" (2007: 14, emphasis in original). So, for example, if a person's having a certain character or set of motives is enough to bring it about that she makes a certain choice, "then to be *ultimately* responsible for the choice, the agent must be at least in part responsible by virtue of choices or actions voluntarily performed in the past for having the character and motives he or she now has" (ibid.).

An immediate concern is that satisfying Kane's "ultimate responsibility condition," or UR, would require the completion of a regress like the one identified in Galen Strawson's Basic Argument. Here is Kane's presentation of the regress problem:

> If we must have formed our present wills (our characters and motives) by earlier voluntary choices or actions, then UR would require that if any of these earlier choices or actions *also* had sufficient causes or motives when we performed *them*, then we must have also been responsible for those earlier sufficient causes or motives by virtue of forming them by *still earlier* voluntary choices or action, and so on backwards indefinitely into our past. (2007: 15)

However, Kane argues that this regress would stop if, as we uncover the causal sources of an action of mine, we encounter a choice that did *not* have a sufficient cause (ibid.: 16). In this case, there would be no sufficient cause for which UR would require that I be responsible. Of course, the choice in question is meant to be *my* choice, so it must have been caused by my reasons, motives, desires, and so on – it's just that, on Kane's view, these causal factors must not have *ensured* that I would make the choice I did. In other words, regress-stopping choices must be caused by, but not causally determined by, a person's reasons, motives, desires, and so on.[4]

For Kane, the most important sort of regress-stopping choices are self-forming choices that mold our characters and shape our subsequent behavior. Once our characters are set, much of our subsequent behavior may be determined, but we can still be ultimately responsible for this determined behavior to the degree that our characters were indeterministically self-formed (Kane 2007: 15).

Kane believes that self-forming choices often "occur at those difficult times of life when we are torn between competing visions of what we should do or become" and it is genuinely undetermined how things will turn out (2007: 26). At these times, we feel the pull of competing reasons and temptations, neither of which is sufficient to determine our choice. As a result, it is undetermined which choice we will make, but, however we choose, we will do so on the basis of reasons that we endorse. As an example, suppose that an ambitious businesswoman – I'll call her Maria – is on her way to an important meeting when she witnesses a mugging (ibid.). Maria is torn between stopping and calling for help and continuing on her way. The first option conflicts with her strong desire to make it to her meeting on time; the second option is contrary to the pull of her conscience. Given her psychological makeup, Maria is sensitive to reasons in favor of both options, and either choice would be explicable in terms of important features of her personality. However, neither set of reasons is sufficient to ensure that she will make one choice or the other.

Kane thinks of someone in Maria's position as trying to make two conflicting choices at once: she is trying both "to make a moral choice and to make a conflicting self-interested choice" (2007: 30). Furthermore, Kane assumes that these two efforts are instantiated in Maria's brain as parallel processes in two neural networks: "The input of one of these neural networks consists in the woman's reasons for acting morally and stopping to help the victim; the input of the other network comprises her ambitious motives for going on to her meeting" (ibid.: 28). Of course, only one of these networks will issue in a choice, and which one will do so is meant to be genuinely undetermined – perhaps it will be the result of "quantum indeterminacies in the firings of individual neurons" (ibid.: 29) – but when a choice is made it will be Maria's doing, according to Kane. When she makes one choice or the other, she will thereby "*make* one set of competing reasons or motives prevail over the others then and there *by deciding*" (ibid.: 26–7).

It will help in assessing Kane's theory to set it in the context of a debate internal to libertarianism. As you may recall from chapter 1, libertarians believe that free will and moral responsibility are not compatible with determinism. Some libertarian theories of agency rely on *agent causation*. We often think of causation as a relation that holds between events: for example, the event of a moral consideration occurring to Maria at a certain time might cause the subsequent event of her deciding to call for help. On agent-causal accounts, however, freely willed human actions are brought about not by previous events, or states of the world, but rather by agents who themselves possess the basic ability to bring about effects in the world. When an agent exercises this causal power, he is not determined to do so, or to exercise it in any particular way, by previous events. Randolph Clarke (2003) provides an excellent account of the varieties of libertarianism; see Roderick Chisholm ([1964] 2003) and Timothy O'Connor (2000) for developments of the agent-causal perspective.

In the contemporary debate, agent-causal theories are often regarded with suspicion because they invoke a causal power that appears not to fit neatly into the natural world (though this appearance has been questioned; see Nelkin 2011: 80–97). The world as studied by the natural sciences seems, for the most part, to be one in which occurrences are causally explained in terms of prior states of the world, but agent causation appears to involve a break in this natural causal order. Kane, by contrast, means to offer us a theory of free will that is potentially fully compatible with the naturalistic story that scientists will ultimately tell us about how the brain works and how human actions arise in the world. For Kane, the entire process by which an agent freely wills an action can be analyzed in terms of event-causal processes in the brain; his view requires only that certain of these events are not *deterministically* caused by prior brain states. For another event-causal libertarian theory of free will, see Laura Ekstrom (2000).

For some, Kane's commitment to naturalism will be appealing, but others may feel that it gives us a deflated picture of human agency. As we saw above, Kane says that Maria will "*make* one set of competing reasons or motives prevail over the others then and there *by deciding*," but on Kane's account her "deciding" is just the outcome of an indeterministic causal process in her brain. From a certain perspective, it might not be clear that we are entitled to describe this process as Maria *making a decision*. It may seem instead that there is simply a certain undetermined occurrence in her brain and that Maria, as an agent, has little to do with this. According to this sort of objection, Kane is giving us a story of what happens *in* an agent, but not a story of an agent doing anything. (For an important account of this sort of worry – though not one directed at Kane's view – see Velleman 1992.) Of course, while this criticism might appeal to advocates of agent causation, it's not likely to appeal to compatibilists about free will and moral responsibility, since they tend to be as comfortable as Kane is with a naturalistic, event-causal picture of human agency.

A different, though related, worry about Kane's view is that the indeterminism in the causal process that leads to Maria's actions *undermines* her control of those actions: perhaps the indeterminism makes the occurrence of her action random or accidental in a way that calls into question her moral responsibility. (The point here is related to the theme of §1.3.) In response, Kane admits that there is an irreducible element of chance in his story of how freely willed actions come about. He notes, for example, that "whether an effort succeeds *does* depend upon whether certain undetermined neurons fire or not; and whether these neurons fire is not under the control of the agent; and we can consequently say it is a matter of chance whether the efforts leading to SFAs [self-forming actions] succeed or not" (2007: 37). However, Kane does not believe that this element of chance diminishes moral responsibility. After all, the explanation for why Maria might make either of two choices is that the reasons in favor of both choices have a genuine pull on her. As Kane puts it, "the indeterminism that is admittedly diminishing [Maria's] control over one thing she is trying to do…*is coming from her own will* – from her desire and effort to do the opposite" (ibid.: 39). The presence of indeterminism is simply what allows Maria to choose in either of two ways, but, whichever she chooses, she will be responsible because she will be choosing for her own reasons. And as Kane notes, "*willing* what you do...for *reasons* that you endorse" is usually what's "required to say something is done 'on purpose,' rather than accidently, capriciously, or merely by chance" (ibid.: 29).

It's not clear that Kane's response entirely disposes of the concerns about the "chanciness" of Maria's choice, but, while a skeptic about moral responsibility might push this worry against Kane, compatibilists ought not to be too interested in doing so. After all, compatibilists typically want free will and moral responsibility to be compatible with either the truth *or the falsity* of determinism. So, like Kane, they should be content with an element of chance in the causal history of a free action. However, what compatibilists *will* question is Kane's insistence that indeterminism is *necessary* for moral responsibility. For the compatibilist, it won't be clear that the presence of indeterminism in the causal process leading to an agent's action increases that agent's control over, or ownership of, the action in a way that could be relevant to moral responsibility.

Suppose that it is causally determined that Maria, after reflecting on the moral reasons in favor of doing so, will stop and call the police when she witnesses a mugging. Now imagine an alternate version of the story in which Maria makes the same decision for the same reasons but that it was also possible that she might have made a different decision. Why should we believe that, in the second version of the story, Maria is morally responsible for her behavior in a way that she is not in the first version? This question is especially pressing when we recall that, on Kane's event-causal indeterministic version of the story, whether Maria makes one choice or another will depend merely on whether certain neurons in her brain happen to fire at a particular time and that this is not something over which she exercises control.

It would help us see how indeterminism could contribute to Maria's moral responsibility if she had direct control over how the indeterministic processes in her brain turned out – as if she could "crawl down to the place where the indeterminism originates (in the individual neurons) and *make* them go one way or the other" (Kane 2007: 37). Yet this is just the sort of fantastic power that Kane does not want to attribute to agents (and if Maria did have this sort of control over her neural processes, it's not clear they would still be indeterministic). The problem is that, on Kane's more realistic account of how choices are formed, it's not obvious that insisting on indeterminism in an agent's neural processes explains how the agent is more responsible for her behavior than she would be if those processes were deterministic.

3.3 Mesh Theories, Manipulation Cases, and Taking Responsibility

As we've just seen, theorists like Robert Kane and Galen Strawson believe that the historical processes that shape us are relevant to our present moral responsibility. However, some approaches to responsibility reject this claim; these views regard moral responsibility as entirely dependent on the way an agent is at the time of action. We've seen that New Attributionist theories tend to have this feature, but the most well-known versions of this sort of view are referred to variously as structural, mesh, or hierarchical theories of responsibility (these are also the Real Self views to which we saw Susan Wolf refer in chapter 2). On this sort of approach, an agent is morally responsible for an action if (roughly) there is a certain sort of "mesh" or fit between how the agent wants to be moved and the desires that actually produce her behavior (the "mesh" terminology comes from Fischer and Ravizza 1998: 184). All that matters for responsibility on this theory is the contemporary structure of an agent's will, and not how that structure came about.

Mesh Theories of Responsibility

The structural approach to moral responsibility is most commonly associated with the work of Harry Frankfurt (also see Dworkin 1970b; Neely 1974; Watson 1975). Frankfurt's famous comparison between a willing and an unwilling drug addict can help us see how the approach is supposed to work ([1971] 1988b). Imagine two addicts who both have a desire – a first-order desire, as Frankfurt puts it – to take the drug to which they are addicted. Assume further that the intense first-order desire to take the drug will ultimately move both addicts to take it. In a sense, then, the will of neither addict is free: both will ultimately choose to take the drug regardless of whether they *really* want to do so (the force of "really" should become clear in a moment).

Now suppose that one of these addicts is *willing*: he is happy to be addicted to his drug. This addict affirms and identifies with his first-order desire for the drug from a higher-order perspective. He has, in other words, a second-order desire for his first-order desire to be effective. So, even though the willing addict lacks one sort of freedom (since he would ultimately be moved to take the drug regardless of whether he endorsed his desire for it), when the willing addict takes the drug, he does so "freely and of his own free will" (Frank-furt [1971] 1988b: 25).

Assuming that we are inclined to regard blame as appropriate in the context of drug use, the willing addict may seem especially blameworthy because he has taken ownership of his addiction by reflectively and wholeheartedly endorsing the addictive desires that move him. Our response to an *unwilling* addict would presumably be different. An unwilling addict takes a stand against, and is alienated from, his addictive desire in a way that might be thought to undermine his moral responsibility for taking the drug (even though when he takes the drug he fulfills one of his first-order desires). Such an addict is, Frankfurt says, "helplessly violated by his own desires" ([1971] 1988b: 17). The source of this violation is internal to the agent, but it is a violation nonetheless because, by taking up a certain higher-order perspective, the addict has defined himself as against the first-order desire that over-whelms him.

But where, we might ask, do our higher-order desires come from? Why, for example, does the willing addict embrace his addictive urges? If we think that the willing addict's behavior is more truly his own because he endorses his desire for the drug, then we might think that his endorsement itself must somehow have acquired the authority to speak for the agent. So we might worry that the higher-order desire itself needs to be authorized from an even higher-order perspective. It might seem that there is no natural way to put an end to this regress, in which case it will be puzzling how we can have genuine ownership of our first-order desires and the actions they inspire (Watson 1975). Frankfurt is unmoved by this sort of worry. He argues that at some point we may simply decisively commit ourselves to, and identify with, a desire or mode of behavior, and at that point, because our commitment is decisive, there is no need to ask whether our commitment is itself endorsed from a higher-order perspective ([1987] 1988c: 167–9).

A related worry is that accounts such as Frankfurt's are incomplete because an agent's will can display the sort of structure or mesh that is supposed to be sufficient for moral responsibility even in cases in which the agent was subjected to pressures (such as brainwashing) that intuitively undermine moral responsibility. If we think that responsibility is undermined in such cases, then the fact that an agent's will displays a certain structure cannot be enough for moral responsibility (Fischer and Ravizza 1998: 196).

Consider, for example, the residents of the fictional community of Walden Two in B. F. Skinner's utopian novel of the same name. The Waldenites are happy and well adjusted, but this is because they have all been subjected to social engineering and behavioral conditioning since birth. Despite having been exposed to such a powerful form of control, the Waldenites do not feel violated or unfree since they can behave precisely as they want. Of course, what a Waldenite wants to do – what he enjoys, desires, and so on – is precisely what the architects of his community have programmed him to want. A Waldenite has been precisely engineered to be just the sort of person that he is, so there is no need to prevent him from acting on his desires and inclinations.

The Waldenites seem to fulfill the conditions on moral responsibility that someone like Frankfurt would propose. Indeed, from one perspective, we might agree with one of Walden Two's planners that it "is the freest place on earth" (Skinner [1948] 1962: 263). On the other hand, we might agree with Robert Kane that there is a "deeper sense" of free will that the Waldenites lack and which goes beyond merely being able to do what you want. "In this deeper sense" of free will, says Kane, the Waldenites' "wills are not 'their own' because they are not the original creators of their own ends or purposes" (1996: 65; for Kane's discussion of *Walden Two*, see ibid.: 65–9, 201–4).

We saw in the last section what Kane thinks would be required for the Waldenites to be the creators of their ends and purposes. Yet, even if we do not agree with Kane that moral responsibility requires ultimate responsibility, we may still think that, in order to be genuinely free and morally responsible, the Waldenites would have to have had more control over their own characters than they in fact had. Or, at the very least, we might think that moral responsibility requires the absence of the sort of manipulation to which the Waldenites were subjected.[5]

A Manipulation Case

Now that we have raised the topic of manipulation, let us turn to Alfred Mele's much discussed manipulation case involving two philosophers: Beth and Ann.

Beth is a philosophy professor but she's not very productive. In fact, the college dean would very much like for Beth to be more like Ann, who is a much more committed and productive philosopher. Thus, the dean arranges for a team of psychologists and neuroscientists to manipulate Beth's brain while she is asleep so that, when she wakes up, she is psychologically identical (in the relevant respects) to Ann. After the brainwashing, when she "reflects on her [new] preferences and values, Beth finds that they fully support a life dedicated to philosophical work, and she wholeheartedly embraces such a life and the collection of values that supports it" (Mele 1995: 145). In other words, Beth satisfies the structural requirements that Frankfurt places on moral responsibility.

The central difference between Ann and Beth is that, whereas Ann's "values were acquired under her own steam," Beth's values "were imposed upon her" (Mele 1995: 155). For Mele, this means that, while Ann and Beth "make equal use of the relevant...values in 'governing' their mental lives," in Beth's case, this is merely "*ersatz* self-government" (ibid.: 156). Beth's self-governance is ersatz (that is, not genuine) because the "dean and his cronies seized control of the direction that her life would take…Behind the facade of self-government, external governors lurk" (ibid.).

Now if Beth is not a genuinely self-governing agent, then, according to most theories, she would not be fully morally responsible for her behavior in the way that Ann is. But is the control that Beth seems to exercise over her behavior after the manipulation merely ersatz self-government? There are several connected concerns here. We might, for example, think that Beth's real values – and therefore the only ones that could inform genuine self-government – are those that she possessed prior to her manipulation. Since Beth no longer has those values, perhaps self-government is impossible for her. Indeed, we may wonder whether the person who confronts us after the manipulation is really Beth at all: perhaps the manipulation has actually created a new person.

While this last question is interesting, the issue of whether Beth's manipulation created a new person can perhaps be put aside for present purposes. Suppose that the person who now answers to the name "Beth" treats you poorly because her intense devotion to philosophy is associated with a lack of concern for how her actions affect other people. We don't necessarily have to determine whether this person – post-manipulation Beth – is the same person as pre-manipulation Beth in order to decide whether it is appropriate for you to blame her for having mistreated you. At least on the New Attributionist approach that I favor, all that would be required for post-manipulation Beth to be open to such blame is that her bad behavior is attributable to her in the sense that it issues from and expresses her objectionable judgments and values.

However, this just brings us back to the question of whether the values that result from the manipulation are *Beth's* values. But, while these values certainly do not belong to pre-manipulation Beth, it's less clear why we should worry that they don't belong to post-manipulation Beth. For example, we might hold the view – which seems plausible to me – that, as long as a set of values play for post-manipulation Beth the action-guiding and action-explaining role that values normally play, those values are hers. If we accept this view, then we may well conclude that post-manipulation Beth is a moral agent in the way that is relevant for moral responsibility: her actions issue from the right kinds of internal states in the right way for them to express interpersonally significant values, attitudes, and judgments about reasons (cf. Vargas 2006: 363ff.).

On the other hand, perhaps the facts about how Beth acquired her new values ought to cast her actions in a different light for us. We might, for example, think that, since Beth did not play a role in acquiring these values, they can't fairly be attributed to her for the purposes of moral appraisal. This is certainly what many people would want to say about a case in which values and desires are *temporarily* induced in an unwilling agent. As T. M. Scanlon puts it, such values wouldn't really belong to the agent, since they would be "just visiting" (1998: 278). However, if Beth's new values are permanent – or perhaps even if they are just long lasting – then we may think: *That's just the way Beth is now.*

No doubt Beth acquired her values in an odd and unfortunate way, but all of us are unfortunate to the degree that we have values and inclinations that lead us to act badly. And while most of us played a sort of role in acquiring our values that Beth did not, it's useful to bear in mind the point of Galen Strawson's Basic Argument: even if we, as normal agents, can make choices that lead us to acquire certain values, we cannot choose the original constitutions in accord with which we make our subsequent value-acquiring choices. And if even normal agents with the best upbringings are not entirely the authors of their own values, then it is not clear that Beth's failure to play this authorial role is incompatible with moral responsibility.

It's also worth considering the possibility that our reluctance to hold Beth morally responsible stems from the worry that doing so is incompatible with acknowledging that, as Michael McKenna puts it, Beth *"was done wrong"* (2004: 183; see Zimmerman 2003 and Talbert 2009a for discussion of the precise ways in which Beth was wronged). Yet it seems clear (as McKenna notes) that there are two separate issues here: Beth was wronged, but acknowledging this does not commit us to denying that she can wrong others in a way for which we might hold her morally responsible.

Of course, what accounts for Beth having been wronged is the fact that she was intentionally manipulated. But suppose that Beth's post-manipulation state was brought about in a different way. If it had been a stroke or an unlucky fall that caused Beth's devotion to philosophy, then she would not have been wronged by anyone. Would this change our assessment of Beth's responsibility? As Nomy Arpaly notes: "Anyone who wishes to argue that Beth is not morally responsible for her actions would need to explain why having been influenced by an evil human being exempts from responsibility in a way that having been irrationally influenced in a similar way by some unlucky chance of a force of nature does not" (2003: 129). Still, it is hard even for a committed attributionist such as myself to fully shake the intuition that Beth's manipulation calls her responsibility into question. For his part, Mele revisits the Beth–Ann case and responds to several criticisms of his original argument in his *Free Will and Luck* (2006).

Taking Responsibility

Recall that compatibilism is the view that free will and moral responsibility are compatible with determinism. Manipulation cases like the one involving Beth are sometimes thought to present particular problems for compatibilist accounts of moral responsibility, at least if we agree that Beth's manipulation means that she is not responsible for her post-manipulation behavior. The problem is that, if determinism wouldn't rule out Beth's moral responsibility, it is not clear why her having been manipulated would do so (a concern along these lines is developed in detail in the next section). Thus, compatibilism may be in the uncomfortable position of not being able to deliver what may seem like the intuitive conclusion in cases like Beth's. One option, of course, is for compatibilists to argue, as I did above, that manipulated agents like Beth really are morally responsible. But if this is too big a bullet for compatibilists to bite, they can try instead to include conditions in their accounts of moral responsibility that exclude manipulated agents from responsibility without giving up central compatibilist commitments.

John Martin Fischer and Mark Ravizza offer the best-known instance of this second strategy. As I noted in chapter 2,

Fischer and Ravizza believe that a person is morally responsible, in the sense of being a proper target of reactive attitudes, if she exercises "guidance control" over her behavior. One thing that's required for guidance control is that an agent's actions issue from a psychological mechanism that is appropriately responsive to reasons (I briefly described this aspect of guidance control in §2.3). In addition, Fischer and Ravizza say that this psychological mechanism must belong to the agent: she must "own" her reasons-responsive psychological mechanism in virtue of having fulfilled the historical condition of *taking responsibility* for that mechanism.

According to Fischer and Ravizza, an agent takes responsibility for his reasons-responsive mechanism if he fulfills the following three conditions:

> First, an individual must see himself as the source of his behavior...[he] must see himself as an agent; he must see that his choices and actions are efficacious in the world.
>
> ...
>
> Second, the individual must accept that he is a fair target of the reactive attitudes as a result of how he exercises this agency in certain contexts.
>
> ...
>
> The third condition on taking responsibility requires that the individual's view of himself specified in the first two conditions be based, in an appropriate way, on the evidence... For example, the child's view of himself as an agent needs to be based...on his experience with the effects of his choices and actions on the world. And his view of himself as an apt target for the reactive attitudes...needs to be based on what his parents have taught him and his broader experiences with the social practices of (say) praise and blame. (1998: 210–13)

The third condition helps Fischer and Ravizza avoid having to say that an agent is responsible for her behavior if she satisfies the first two conditions only as a result of having been manipulated in the way that Beth was. On their account, a person who was manipulated in this way would not be morally responsible because her belief that she is a fair target of the reactive attitudes would not have been formed in the appropriate way (ibid.: 236).

Additionally, a manipulated agent is unlikely to have taken responsibility for the specific mechanism that issues in her post-manipulation action. To take Fischer and Ravizza's example, suppose that a neuroscientist manipulates Judith's brain so that she has a strong desire to punch a friend of hers (1998: 232–5). While Judith, as a normal adult, has presumably taken responsibility for her normal reasons-responsive mechanism and the actions that issue from it, Fischer and Ravizza argue that, since "Judith does not know about the manipulation" she suffered, she "has *not* taken responsibility for the kind of mechanism that actually issues in" her punching her friend (ibid.: 233). But suppose that Judith discovers how she came to have her new and uncharacteristic desire to punch her friend. In this case, Fischer and Ravizza say that she would be in a position to "modify her desire" or she might "decide to keep her new desire" (ibid.: 235). Either way, she would now be responsible for her behavior because she would now grasp the mechanism from which it issues.

There are several points to make here. First, let's suppose that, for some reason, Judith decides to keep her new desire. This would be odd, since the desire to punch her friend is supposed to be inconsistent with Judith's pre-manipulation psychology. In fact, we might think that her endorsement of the new desire must have something to do with the fact that she was manipulated. If this were indeed the case, then Fischer and Ravizza would want to deny that Judith could really take responsibility for her behavior, since they need to resist the possibility that responsibility can arise out of manipulation in this way (1998: 235–6). But this leads to a strange consequence. Suppose that Judith can never genuinely take responsibility for her new desire because her inclination to do so arises from her manipulation. In this case, she might go through life acting happily, intentionally, and in a perfectly normal way on desires that she received long ago, and yet she is never morally responsible for her actions. At some point, I suspect that we would be inclined to regard Judith as morally responsible simply because she acts on her desires in the normal way. But in this case, we might as well regard her as responsible immediately after her manipulation, if that is the point at which she begins to act on her new desire in the normal way.

We might also question the premise that Judith needs to be aware of the fact that she was manipulated if she is to take responsibility for her new desires and subsequent behavior. In this vein, Neil Levy says,

> it is implausible that we need to understand either the causes or the details of the implementation of our action-generating mechanisms in order to take responsibility for them. Agents *routinely* fail to understand the causes of their desires; with regard to many of them, the stories they tell themselves are false. Many of our motivating desires we acquired in the dim past, in early childhood, and their origins are lost to us. (Levy 2011b: 105; cf. Pereboom 2001: 121)

As Levy sees it, someone like Judith (or Beth) might wake up, notice that she has a new desire, and not see any reason to distinguish between her responsibility for acting on this new desire and her responsibility for acting on her pre-existing desires (2011b: 104). She may not know where her new desire came from, but that wouldn't give her any reason to question her responsibility for acting on it.

For Levy, this means that Fischer and Ravizza haven't added anything to their compatibilist story that rules out the responsibility of a manipulated agent like Judith. Levy sees this as a problem, since he believes that such manipulated agents are not morally responsible. For my own part, I think Fischer and Ravizza should say that Judith owns her behavior in the way required for moral responsibility as long as she acts consistently with her values and desires and for reasons that she counts in favor of so acting. If this is the case, then, on my view, Judith's behavior belongs to her in the way required for moral assessment regardless of where her values and desires came from.

3.4 The Four-Case Argument

I'll close this chapter by introducing another manipulation argument that's meant to cause trouble for compatibilism: Derk Pereboom's four-case argument. Pereboom has offered several versions of this argument (1995, 2001, 2007, 2014); I'll focus on the version in his important book *Living Without Free Will* (2001).

Pereboom's argument supports the following incompatibilist intuition: "if all of our behavior were 'in the cards' before we were born – in the sense that things happened before we came to exist that, by way of a deterministic causal process, inevitably result in our behavior – then we cannot legitimately be blamed for our wrongdoing" (2001: 6; cf. ibid.: 89). The argument begins with the presentation of a case in which an agent satisfies compatibilist conditions on moral responsibility and yet has been subjected to manipulation that intuitively undermines responsibility. Next, Pereboom appeals to a series of intermediate cases aiming to show that there is no basis for thinking that the manipulated agent just introduced is different from a causally determined agent in terms of moral responsibility. Thus, if we accept that the manipulated agent is not responsible, the same conclusion should apply to a determined agent.

In each of Pereboom's cases, Professor Plum kills Ms White in order to achieve some selfish end. Plum satisfies several compatibilist conditions on responsibility: he acts from characteristic desires upon which he wants to act but that are not irresistible in any normal sense. Additionally, Plum's desires are modifiable in light of "his rational consideration of the relevant reasons" (2001: 111). Finally, while Plum acts for selfish reasons, "he is not completely egoistic"; "he retains the general capacity to grasp, apply, and regulate his behavior by moral reasons" and, in virtue of this capacity, he is able "to revise and develop his moral character over time" (ibid.).

In Case 1, Plum is "created by neuroscientists, who can manipulate him directly through the use of radio-like technology" (Pereboom 2001: 112). The scientists are in direct control of Plum's reasoning processes and, when he confronts the situation involving Ms White, they operate their radio-like technology, "causing his reasoning process to be rationally egoistic," with the result that Plum decides to kill White for selfish reasons (ibid.: 113). This decision is characteristic for Plum, "since he is often manipulated to be rationally egoistic" (ibid.). Additionally, while Plum identifies with the desires that lead him to kill White, they are not irresistible: had certain features of his situation been different, he would have reached a different conclusion about what to do.

It's hard not to accept Pereboom's claim that Plum is not responsible in Case 1: he seems too much a puppet of the scientists to be genuinely blameworthy for killing Ms White. Case 2 moves us closer to the everyday situation of a causally deterministic world. In this case, neuroscientists create Plum but they do not control his reasoning directly. Instead, they "have programmed him to weigh reasons for action so that he is often but not exclusively rationally egoistic" (Pereboom 2001: 113–14). While Plum is not programmed always to act on egoistic reasons, in the case of Ms White, his programming is such that "he is causally determined to undertake" the same reasoning process described in Case 1 with the same result (ibid.: 114). Do we feel any better about Plum's chances for moral responsibility in this case? Does moving from a case of direct control of his reasoning to a pre-programmed reasoning process make any difference?

In Case 3, neuroscientists no longer create Plum; he is simply raised in a cultural context that instills the same rationally egoistic reasoning processes described above. He has been exposed to rigorous training – to which he did not consent and over which he had no control – with the result that, as an adult, and when confronted with the circumstances involving Ms White, it is causally determined that he will choose to kill her. At this point, of course, we have left the realm of science fiction. There are no neuroscientists controlling Plum's reasoning directly or even by programming, but, if his decision is still determined by prior causal factors over which he had no control, are we any more inclined to judge that he is open to moral blame?

In Case 4, Plum is just a normal person; nothing about his generation or upbringing is remarkable. However, causal determinism is true in this case: every step of Plum's reasoning process is, like every other event in the world, causally determined to be precisely what it is. This does not mean that he acts on an irresistible desire when he decides to kill Ms White for selfish reasons – had the circumstances surrounding his choice been different, then he might have made a different choice, but given what the circumstances were, his choice to kill was determined by factors beyond his control.

Pereboom believes that the best explanation for why Plum is not morally responsible in Cases 1–3 "is that his action results from a deterministic causal process that traces back to factors beyond his control" (2001: 116). Since precisely this circumstance obtains in Case 4 as well, Pereboom concludes that Plum is not responsible in Case 4 either. But what is true of Plum will be true of anyone in a deterministic world, so determinism is not compatible with moral responsibility. (Pereboom combines this argument with criticisms of event-causal and agent-causal libertarian approaches to achieve a more general skepticism about free will and moral responsibility.)

Pereboom's argument does an excellent job of highlighting one of the central issues of this chapter: namely, the worry that, if our exercises of agency are ultimately determined by factors beyond our control, we are not the sources of our actions in the right way to support ascriptions of moral responsibility. (Since Pereboom questions the compatibility of sourcehood and determinism, he advocates *source incompatibilism* rather than *leeway incompatibilism*, which denies the compatibility of access to alternatives – that is, leeway – and determinism; Pereboom 2014: 4.) Of course, there are replies that might be made to Pereboom. Most obvious are concerns about the way Plum's mental states in Case 1 are directly produced moment to moment by external agents. Despite Pereboom's assurances, we may worry that, once the case is sufficiently fleshed out, we will see that Plum's agency is undermined by these invasive manipulations in ways that call his responsibility into question independently of the issue of determinism. This may give the compatibilist room to explain why Plum is not morally responsible in Case 1, even though he is responsible in the other cases that don't feature the same sort of manipulation. As Pereboom himself summarizes this general sort of objection (in a recent reconsideration of his original argument), many critics have argued that, in Case 1, "Plum fails to satisfy intuitive conditions on agency because he is too disconnected from reality, or because he himself lacks ordinary agential control, or because he is not an agent at all" (ibid.: 76).

Call the above a "soft-line" approach to the four-case argument. Alternatively, we might take the hard-line approach advocated by Michael McKenna (2008). On this approach, the compatibilist accepts that Plum is responsible in Case 4 and maintains that, if Plum can truly be said to satisfy compatibilist conditions on responsibility in all the other cases, we should simply accept that he is responsible in those cases as well. As Kristin Demetriou (2010) points out, the compatibilist can exploit the synergy between soft- and hard-line approaches to present Pereboom with a dilemma: either Plum in Case 1 is (to echo Pereboom's language) an agent in a robust sense – he's in touch with reality and exercises agential control over his behavior – in which case the compatibilist can comfortably take a hard line even in Case 1, or he doesn't meet this description, in which case the soft-line approach seems viable.

In his recent book *Free Will, Agency, and Meaning in Life* (2014), Pereboom responds to the above criticisms (and many others besides) and offers a refined version of his position. Of particular interest is an adjustment made to Case 1 of the four-case argument. In the revised version, instead of neuroscientists exercising moment-to-moment control over Plum, we are to imagine that "the manipulators enhance Plum's disposition to reason self-interestedly at the requisite time, so that they know that as a result it is causally ensured that he will decide to murder White and that he will want so to decide" (Pereboom 2014: 76; cf. Shabo 2010: 376). The interference of the neuroscientists might be analogous, Pereboom suggests, to the way that "[f]inding out that the home team lost can cause one to reason and behave more egoistically and less charitably" (2014: 76).

This revised version of Case 1 is supposed to give us a manipulation that "preserve[s] satisfaction of intuitive conditions on agency" and yet also "render[s] it plausible that Plum is not morally responsible" (Pereboom 2014: 76). Of course, as I suggested above, insofar as a compatibilist agrees that the conditions of agency are intact in this case, it will be correspondingly easier for her to take a hard-line approach to the argument. After all, a compatibilist is unlikely to conclude that a person is not morally responsible just because he found out that the home team lost and this made him act more egoistically, so perhaps we should draw a similar conclusion about the neuroscientists' intervention. Ultimately, this raises delicate issues about the degree to which it is permissible to bring compatibilist-friendly intuitions to bear in our analysis of the four-case argument – a subject to which Pereboom gives detailed attention (ibid.: 91–9).

3.5 Conclusion

As we saw in the last chapter (§2.4), some philosophers believe that agents who experienced certain forms of deprivation as children might not be morally responsible for their behavior as adults. This chapter has brought certain aspects of this concern into sharper focus: given that we are shaped by forces beyond our control, perhaps we are not morally responsible for the behavior to which these forces ultimately give rise. Indeed, and as Thomas Nagel emphasizes, as moral agents, we are at the mercy of fate in numerous ways: not only do we lack control over the forces that shape us, we often lack control over the moral problems that confront us and even over the causal outcomes of many of our actions.

The preceding concerns present challenges for theories of moral responsibility, though I have argued that some of these can be met head-on by denying, insofar as it is possible, the relevance of personal history for moral responsibility. All that matters for responsibility, I have suggested, is how a person is now, the nature and moral quality of her present behavior, and the current control she exercises over this behavior. However, as we have seen, taking this line is not without costs; for one thing, it can lead us to embrace conclusions that seem implausible to many people, such as that a manipulated agent such as Beth/Ann is morally responsible. As an alternative, we might try to include historical conditions in our theory of moral responsibility that exclude the responsibility of manipulated agents (and perhaps of people with certain sorts of upbringings). A third option, of course, would be to embrace some form of skepticism about moral responsibility: perhaps genuine moral responsibility requires the fulfillment of conditions that generally are not – and perhaps cannot be – fulfilled.

Early on in the next chapter we will encounter additional reflections on the significance of personal history for moral responsibility, but the focus there will be on how a person's history can undermine her ability to tell right from wrong.

3.6   Further Reading

A number of papers on moral luck are collected in Statman (1993); unfortunately, this volume can be difficult to find. Dana Nelkin's (2013) *Stanford Encyclopedia of Philosophy* article on moral luck is a valuable and readily available resource. In discussing moral luck, I noted that most of us have never faced the moral tests to which ordinary citizens of Nazi Germany were subjected. This observation is made more acute when we take into account evidence from social psychology which suggests that people are much more likely to be obedient to authority than we ordinarily suppose: see Doris (2002) and Milgram (1969). Doris's account considers how the data from psychology intersects with concerns about moral responsibility; also see Nelkin (2005) and Vargas (2013) on this subject. One topic that I did not develop here, but that would have fit well in this chapter, has to do with the relationship between personal identity and moral responsibility (particularly in the context of examples such as the Beth/Ann case); for valuable work on this subject, see Khoury (2013), Matheson (2014), and Shoemaker (2012). In addition to the skeptical outlooks defended by Levy, Pereboom, and Galen Strawson, readers should see Smilansky (2000) and Waller (2011).

4
Competence, Conversation, and Blame

A premise that many important accounts of moral responsibility share is that wrongdoers are open to serious moral
blame only if they could have recognized and responded
appropriately to the moral considerations that counted
against their bad behavior.[6] There is, in other words, commonly thought to be a *moral competence requirement* on
blame (a similar requirement might also apply to praise but,
as usual, blame takes the spotlight). Wrongdoers who meet
this requirement could have recognized that their behavior
was wrong and could have given this consideration its proper
weight in deciding how to behave.

Moral competence, or the lack of it, can be general or
specific. Some agents, such as psychopaths, appear to be
generally morally incompetent. They are, in other words,
globally impaired for responsiveness to moral reasons. Other
agents may suffer from localized impairments of moral competence: for one reason or another, it is impossible, or at least
very difficult, for them to discern and respond appropriately
to a subset of moral considerations.

Since it has seemed so natural to so many philosophers to
assume some version of the moral competence requirement
on blame, I will give special attention in the next section to
considerations in favor of rejecting this requirement.

4.1   Moral Competence and the Fairness of Blame

I'll begin by discussing agents with local impairments of moral competence. These agents are often depicted as the products of a bad upbringing that warped their moral values, making it difficult for them to be appropriately sensitive to moral considerations. Unlike psychopaths, these agents are not entirely immune to moral considerations; instead, they have "blind spots" of varying size when it comes to recognizing the force of moral reasons. As we will see, it is easier to make the case that agents with moral blind spots are blameworthy than it is to make the same case with respect to psychopaths.

It's worth bearing in mind that a bad upbringing is not necessary for an agent to suffer from the kinds of impairments about to be discussed. Presumably, it's possible for a person to have had the best upbringing in the world and still turn out to be someone who has difficulty responding appropriately to moral considerations.

The Case of JoJo

A good place to start is with Susan Wolf's example of JoJo, who is a person with a very wide moral blind spot indeed. It's tempting, in fact, to think of him as a psychopath, though I don't think this is accurate (for reasons that I'll indicate shortly). JoJo was raised by his father, the evil dictator of a small, unnamed country. Despite being deeply evil and sadistic, JoJo's father dotes on the boy (after a fashion). Thus,

> JoJo is given a special education and is allowed to accompany his father and observe his daily routine. In light of this treatment, it is not surprising that little JoJo takes his father as a role model and develops values very much like Dad's. As an adult, he does many of the same sorts of things his father did, including sending people to prison or to death or to torture chambers on the basis of whim. He is not *coerced* to

do these things, he acts according to his own desires. More-over, these are desires he wholly *wants* to have. When he steps back and asks, "Do I really want to be this sort of person?" his answer is resoundingly "Yes," for this way of life expresses a crazy sort of power that forms part of his deepest ideal. (Wolf 1987: 53–4)

Wolf concludes, not unreasonably, that, "[i]n light of JoJo's heritage and upbringing...it is dubious at best that he should be regarded as responsible for what he does" (ibid.: 54). After all, anyone who had the same sort of upbringing would prob-ably have become "twisted and perverse" in just the way JoJo is (ibid.).

There's a lot going on in the quoted passage. For one thing, Wolf means to give us a case in which a bad actor fulfills the *structural* requirements on moral responsibility introduced in the previous chapter (§3.3). JoJo fulfills these requirements because he is exactly the sort of person he wants to be and is moved by desires that he is entirely happy to be moved by. If JoJo is not morally responsible for his behavior, then this shows that the satisfaction of structural requirements is not enough for moral responsibility. So perhaps one thing to take away from the JoJo example is that – as we saw several authors argue in the last chapter – facts about a per-son's history can undermine that person's present moral responsibility.

There's certainly something to be said for this interpreta-tion of Wolf's example. She clearly believes that it is unfair to blame a person for his bad behavior if his upbringing makes it unreasonable to expect him to be anything other than "twisted and perverse" as an adult. However, Wolf's point goes deeper than this. For example, she knows that, since none of us has much control over our upbringing, insist-ing that such control is necessary for moral responsibility can – as demonstrated in the last chapter – put us on the path to skepticism. Wolf is no skeptic about moral responsibility, so she needs to explain JoJo's lack of moral responsibility by citing considerations that don't apply to most other people. But this is easy enough: not only was JoJo's upbringing worse than average, it also seems to have damaged him in a particu-lar way.

In Wolf's terms, JoJo suffers from a sort of (moral) insanity. Sanity, as Wolf construes it, involves "the ability to know the difference between right and wrong, and a person who [like JoJo], even on reflection, cannot see that having someone tortured because he failed to salute you is wrong plainly lacks the requisite ability" (1987: 56). So, on Wolf's account, it is JoJo's lack of sanity – his inability to tell right from wrong, at least in some cases – that ultimately explains why he is not morally responsible for his behavior.

As Wolf points out, similar conclusions can presumably be drawn about groups such as "the slaveowners of the 1850s, the Nazis of the 1930s, and many male chauvinists of our fathers' generation" (1987: 56–7). Like JoJo, members of these groups were often raised in circumstances that fostered bad moral values in them, and their possession of these values may often have made it difficult for them to recognize the true moral status of some of their behavior. More clearly than in the case of JoJo, these people are not psychopaths (indeed, one reason I don't interpret JoJo as a psychopath is that Wolf means for his case to shed light on the status of wrongdoers who are clearly not psychopaths). The average slave-owner, for example, was presumably capable of engaging with *some* moral considerations, but this is compatible with a slave-owner, through no fault of his own, having great difficulty recognizing the moral impermissibility of slavery. And, according to Wolf, "[i]f we think that the agents [JoJo, Nazis, slave-owners, etc.] could not help but be mistaken about their values" – if we believe that their upbringings or social contexts impaired them in this way – "we do not blame them for the actions those values inspired" (ibid.: 57).

Fairness and the Ability to Avoid Blame

Wolf's JoJo example suggests that the pressures that shape agents' values and moral beliefs can impair their moral competence in a way that undermines moral responsibility. On account of a bad upbringing or corrupting social influences a person may come (through no fault of her own) to believe that certain other people are open to treatment that is in fact impermissible. If a person does have such false beliefs, then it may not be reasonable to expect her to respond appropriately to certain moral considerations because her false beliefs do not permit her accurately to assess these considerations. And a person of whom it is not reasonable to expect good behavior is perhaps not an appropriate candidate for moral blame.

Of course, we might question the degree to which a bad upbringing (or other factors) can undermine a person's moral capacities. At any rate, it's certainly true that, for any individual bad actor, it may be very difficult to determine the degree to which he had the capacity to recognize the moral status of his behavior and the force of the reasons that counted against it. Perhaps some wrongdoers, even those raised in the most unfavorable conditions, retain this capacity but simply fail to exercise it. I propose, however, that we set this worry aside and simply grant, for the sake of argument, that some wrongdoers, given their psychological makeup at the time of action, could not reasonably have been expected to respond appropriately to the moral considerations that confronted them. If we grant this assumption, then the question remains whether these wrongdoers are really excused or exempted from moral blame and, if so, why? (If you don't grant the assumption just mentioned, then you won't think that the agents in question have impaired moral competence, so you probably won't be too concerned that their moral responsibility is called into question.)

One reason for thinking that moral competence matters for moral responsibility has to do with the harsh treatment meted out to wrongdoers. Being the target of moral blame, not to mention punishment, is unpleasant. And isn't it unfair to treat people in unpleasant ways if they didn't have a reasonable opportunity to avoid being treated that way? Of course, a central way of avoiding moral blame is to avoid wrongdoing, and a person with impaired moral competence will have difficulty doing this because she will have difficulty appreciating the moral reasons in favor of doing so. So perhaps we should not blame a person who cannot respond appropriately to moral considerations, because it is unfair to blame someone who could not have avoided – or who would have had significant difficulty avoiding – blame. R. Jay Wallace offers a particularly forceful argument along these lines in chapter 7 of *Responsibility and the Moral Sentiments* (1996); also see Erin Kelly (2013) and Neil Levy (2009).

Responding to the Fairness Argument

The line of reasoning just sketched has a lot of intuitive appeal, and something like it no doubt partly explains why so many philosophers believe that moral responsibility requires moral competence. Of course, there are also ways of thinking about moral responsibility that make its dependence on moral competence less certain. For the next few pages, I'll focus on reasons for rejecting the moral competence requirement.

Proponents of the New Attributionist perspective that I outlined in earlier chapters believe (roughly) that the fairness of blaming responses such as resentment has mainly to do with the attributability of wrongdoing to an agent and not necessarily with that agent's ability to avoid wrongdoing.[7] Pamela Hieronymi defends a position like this in "The Force and Fairness of Blame," where she argues that attitudes such as resentment are simply ways of registering the fact that another person has shown us ill will: these attitudes "are *simply* reactions to – that is, they simply mark or acknowledge – the importance of a display of ill will or disregard" (2004: 135). Similarly, Justin D'Arms and Daniel Jacobson, in the context of developing a theory of emotions, have argued that resentment is a "moralized" form of anger that is characterized by a thought along the lines of "I was wronged" (2003). But if resentment is simply a natural response to the judgment that one was wronged or treated with ill will, then perhaps we should conclude with Hieronymi that "adopting the reactive attitudes could be rendered unfair only by considerations that bear on the content of the judgments they reveal" (2004: 133). In other words, my resentment of you would be unfair or inappropriate only if in fact you did not treat me with ill will. And since facts about a person's upbringing, her impaired moral competence, or her difficulty avoiding wrongdoing do not tend to undermine an attribution of ill will, they also don't tend to make a person an inappropriate target of moral blame.

Some of the appeal of the idea that it is unfair to blame those who cannot avoid being blamed may arise from a tendency to conflate various ways in which it can be difficult for a person to avoid an action. Suppose that someone injures you because she was coerced into doing so by a credible threat, or because she was sleepwalking, or because she was subject to an overwhelming compulsion that forced her to act as she did. These are fairly clear cases in which blame would be unfair, and these are also cases in which (in different ways) the agent in question could not reasonably have been expected to avoid her behavior. However, in these cases we don't need to cite the agent's difficulty in avoiding her behavior in order to explain why it would be unfair to blame her. The more basic reason for the unfairness of blame is that the compulsive agent, for example, does not control her behavior in accordance with her judgments about how to behave (and, as I explained in §1.5, a different but importantly related point applies to coerced agents).

But now consider an agent who has difficulty in avoiding wrongdoing, but not because of any difficulty he has controlling his behavior as he sees fit. My suggestion is that it is much less clear that it is unfair to blame such an agent. Take JoJo's case. Let us grant that, given his moral values, JoJo cannot refrain from an act of torture on the basis of recognizing that there are good moral reasons to refrain. But this does not mean that his behavior is out of his control in any normal sense. For example, it is quite compatible with the description just given that JoJo chooses to refrain from an act of torture because he needs to spend time planning a new wave of terror to quell political dissent in his country. Moreover, when he does engage in torture, he acts (as Wolf's description makes clear) just as he wants to act, and his actions express his considered judgments about how other people may be treated. The judgments expressed by JoJo's behavior are, of course, objectionable to his victims, and I suggest that they are objectionable in just the way that reasonably provokes blaming responses.

We should conclude, then, that, while some types of interference with moral competence (such as compulsion) undermine blameworthiness, not all of them do. In particular, the types of interference most often referred to in this debate –

cases in which it is an agent's possession of bad values that interferes with his moral functioning – will not necessarily undermine an agent's blameworthiness. JoJo's commitment to his objectionable values – for example, his commitment to the view that others may be tortured as the mood strikes him – may make it very difficult for him to see that he has reason not to treat others in certain ways, but I can't see why this sort of difficulty should make it inappropriate for JoJo's victims to blame him when he deliberately treats them in ways to which he knows they object.

Praise and Blame

One thing to think about in assessing the moral competence requirement is whether it applies equally to praise and blame. Consider Dana Nelkin's example – similar to one described by Susan Wolf – involving two women named Rosa and Sylvia. As a result of having the same values and motivations, and of responding appropriately to the same moral reasons, both women choose to save a drowning child. However, while Sylvia could have responded differently to the moral reasons in play, Rosa could not have. Given Rosa's psychology, she literally could not have responded to the moral situation differently than she did; Wolf suggests that someone like Rosa may lack "the ability to do otherwise simply because her understanding of the situation is so good and her moral commitment so strong" (1990: 82).

Presumably, Sylvia is praiseworthy for her behavior, but is Rosa? Nelkin says that she is, because her decision-making process is meant to be as similar to Sylvia's as possible: "Rosa acts for precisely the same clear reasons that Sylvia does: she sees a child drowning and realizes that the child's death is an easily preventable...and terrible, terrible thing" (2011: 40). Perhaps Rosa's concern for the child was so deep that she could not have made any other choice, but that doesn't change the nature of her action or the quality of her will, so it doesn't affect her praiseworthiness.

Nelkin's analysis of praiseworthiness seems just right to me: it depends entirely on the quality of the agent's will in acting, not on whether she might have acted with a different sort of will. However, if we applied the same analysis to blame, we would conclude that an agent is blameworthy solely on account of the quality of his will, the reasons he actually responded to, and what this reveals about his orientation toward other people. But Nelkin argues that blameworthiness requires more than this. On her view, it also requires the ability to respond appropriately to moral considerations. So, to build on a suggestion of Nelkin's, even if we knew that a particular soldier had deliberately and willingly targeted a group of civilians out of ethnic hatred, this would not be enough to hold the soldier morally responsible for his war crimes. In addition, we would need "to determine the extent to which soldiers have the ability to recognize and act on good reasons at the moment in question" (Nelkin 2011: 11).[8]

As I've said, many responsibility theorists are inclined toward an opinion like Nelkin's, but I'm not sure that hers is the correct conclusion to draw. To see why, consider another case involving Sylvia and Rosa, except that, this time, instead of doing something good, they do something very bad: suppose that they both decide to drown a young nephew in order to receive an immense inheritance. However, while Sylvia could have responded differently to the incentives created by the possibility of receiving the inheritance, Rosa could not have. Rosa is so devoted to her own selfish ends, and the amount of money involved is so large, that coming to the conclusion that drowning her nephew is *not* the thing to do wasn't a psychologically plausible outcome for her (which is not to say that her action was compulsive or that she couldn't have made a different choice under different circumstances). Whereas, in Nelkin's case, Rosa can't help but act on good reasons because she is so good, in my case, she can't help but act on bad reasons because she is so bad.

Supposing that Sylvia and Rosa are as I described them, is there reason to think that Sylvia would be open to blame but that Rosa would not be? Both of them knowingly, intentionally, and (let us assume) after a period of reflection decide to commit murder for selfish reasons. Making a different choice might not have been psychologically open to Rosa, but that's just because of her overwhelming selfishness and the appeal that the reasons in favor of murder have for her. Why should this explanation of Rosa's inability to behave better be a barrier to moral blame? Another way to put the point is to say that, even if we added to Rosa's story the stipulation that she could have responded to her situation in a morally better way, it is not obvious that we would be adding anything that would clearly change her from being a non-blameworthy agent to a blameworthy one.

On my view, Rosa's blameworthiness is sufficiently explained by referencing the morally bad motives, values, and judgments that *actually* informed her behavior and without having to consider whether certain counterfactual evaluative and volitional outcomes were open to her. (The way I've phrased the point here is meant to recall the discussion of Frankfurt-style compatibilism at the end of chapter 1.)

The Victim's Perspective

Taking up the perspective of a person victimized by a morally impaired wrongdoer can, I think, help us appreciate some of the costs of imposing a moral competence requirement on blame.

Neil Levy argues that "cultural membership can be ethically disabling" and, in order to motivate this claim, he considers a hypothetical member of a slave-owning society (2003: 160; cf. Benson 2001). I'll call Levy's hypothetical slave-owner Scarlet. As Levy points out, Scarlet would probably have "been taught by everyone she most loves and respects – her parents and other close relatives, her teachers, the authorities in her society – that slaves are (say) subhuman" (2003: 152). Of course, the slaves in Scarlet's society would likely have had a different opinion, but, even if Scarlet were aware of this, how should we expect her to respond? Levy argues that, even "if a slave tells her otherwise" – that is, that slaves are *not* subhuman – Scarlet "ought, rationally, to give the views which have been inculcated in her, and which are held by those who... [she believes] are the wisest members of her culture, greater weight than the view of someone she at least suspects of being subhuman" (ibid.).

Levy might be right about this: perhaps it's not reasonable to expect Scarlet to recognize the moral standing of her slaves because it would not be subjectively rational for her to do so. Certainly we can interpret this as an impairment of her moral competence, but how should we expect a slave to respond to Scarlet when she treats him as if he were subhuman, when she rejects his claim to moral standing, ignores his welfare, and uses him merely as a tool for her own purposes? Should we expect the fact that she sincerely believes that slaves are subhuman, and the fact that she is not at fault for having this belief, to quell the slave's moral outrage or to silence his (perhaps unexpressed) resentment and demands for respect?

I suspect that few people would want to answer "yes" to the last question. One way to avoid giving this answer is to say that, while it is unreasonable to expect a mistreated slave to forego blame, and that the slave's blame is entirely understandable, it's still true that Scarlet is not, strictly speaking, a proper target of moral blame. On this perspective, blame is in a way allowed in the slave's case, but only as a concession to human frailty. I don't think this reply goes far enough. Blaming responses on the part of Scarlet's slave are not merely understandable, they are (on my view) entirely appropriate, and I worry that to say otherwise asks the slave to misconstrue the treatment he has received. Scarlet, we may assume, willingly treats her slaves in ways that she knows they do not want to be treated, and she believes that this is acceptable because she does not regard slaves as having the standing to object to such treatment. To say that blame is appropriate in this case is just to say that it is appropriate for Scarlet's actions toward the slave to have the significance for him that intentional and morally offensive behavior usually has for people. By contrast, to say that the slave cannot appropriately blame Scarlet asks him to respond to the treatment he receives as if it were morally analogous to an involuntarily, accidentally, or justifiably imposed harm. I fear, in other words, that, if we say that blame is not an appropriate response for the slave, we risk losing our grip on the moral status and significance of the treatment he received.

Much of what I have said so far depends on attributing a morally condemnable quality of will to Scarlet. This certainly seems plausible to me, but thinking of Scarlet as simply having mistaken beliefs about some moral issues can obscure this point. After all, as the result of a bad education I might mistakenly believe that some types of people – members of a certain ethnic group or nationality – are less intelligent or less hardworking than others, and it might be possible for me to hold these beliefs without having any notable ill will toward members of this group. Similarly, a person who thinks that non-human animals are subhuman probably doesn't have *contempt* for cows or pigs even if he thinks that, in virtue of the fact that they are subhuman, it is permissible to eat these animals, among other unpleasant ways of treating them. Might Scarlet's belief that her slaves are subhuman be like this?

I suspect not. Scarlet's beliefs about her slaves are very different from a superficially similar belief that a person might have about non-human animals (though I don't want to dismiss the idea that many of us are blameworthy for treating animals the way we do). For one thing, Scarlet's belief is presumably immune to a great deal of striking evidence that her slaves are *not* subhuman and that they have intellectual and emotional lives similar to her own. To be clear, the point here is not that Scarlet is blameworthy because she ought to have reformed her beliefs in the face of this evidence. Instead, I want to apply an observation of Nomy Arpaly's: namely, that the recalcitrance of Scarlet's beliefs in the face of evidence to the contrary suggests that her beliefs are held in place by deep-seated attitudes of contempt (2003: 101–11). Now Scarlet may be no more at fault for having these attitudes than she is for having her beliefs about slaves' moral standing. But while she may not be at fault for having the attitudes she has, having these attitudes is a fault in her, and one that it is reasonable for her slaves to respond to with (I claim) the responses involved in moral blame.

I've gone on for a while describing the grounds on which one might reject the moral competence condition on blame, so it's only fair to end this section by posing some difficult questions for the view I have elaborated. If we grant the (admittedly controversial) assumption that someone like Scarlet really can't be expected to recognize her slaves' moral standing, then isn't it inappropriate to demand that she do so? And isn't moral blame really an expression of our moral demands and an attempt to get wrongdoers to see things our way? So doesn't an impairment of moral competence undermine blameworthiness by interfering with the degree to which blame can achieve its ends? I'll take up these questions in §4.3 below.

4.2 Psychopathy

I turn now to the moral responsibility of psychopaths. The scientific literature on psychopathy is vast and on many issues there is a lack of consensus. There is disagreement about the causes of psychopathy; the relationship between psychopathy, sociopathy, and anti-social personality disorder; and the precise diagnostic criteria for the disorder (though see the Further Reading section below for some guidance). Still, there is agreement on the most notable feature of psychopaths: they are persistent wrongdoers whose behavior is characterized by egocentricity, lack of empathy, aggression, impulsivity, and lack of remorse, among other negative personality attributes. Of course, even with respect to these characteristics psychopaths can differ from one another. One of the most widely used tools for diagnosing psychopathy is Robert Hare's Revised Psychopathy Checklist (PCL-R), which grades subjects on a scale (with a score of 40 being the highest possible and a score of 30 often regarded as sufficient for a diagnosis of psychopathy); thus, one person might exhibit psychopathic traits and tendencies to a greater or lesser degree than another. Additionally, while many psychopaths run afoul of the law, it appears that some individuals who would score high on the PCL-R are capable of conducting themselves so as to escape the notice of legal authorities. Some of these "successful psychopaths" are thought to have made their way quite well in the world of business, which suggests that pronounced egotism and a lack of empathy can have their uses in certain occupations (Hare 1993: 102–23; Babiak and Hare 2006). At any rate, Robert Hare and his colleagues claim that there is evidence that "a high level of psychopathic traits does not necessarily impede progress and advancement in corporate organizations" (Babiak et al. 2010: 192).

From the standpoint of assessing moral responsibility, the interesting thing about psychopaths is that their tendency to act badly is associated with significant difficulty responding to moral considerations appropriately. This may mean that psychopaths, at least of the more extreme (and perhaps somewhat idealized) variety, are not simply bad actors – they don't just occasionally fail to attend to moral reasons in the way that any of us might – they may be *incapable* of being good actors, of seeing what morally they ought to do and of doing it because it is the right thing to do.

Now we might wonder whether the psychopath's problems responding to moral reasons have to do mainly with a failure of moral understanding or with a failure of moral motivation. Presumably psychopaths know (in some sense) that theft, murder, and rape are wrong: they know, for example, that performing these acts can get one into trouble with the law. So perhaps psychopaths have a form of moral understanding but are simply not motivated by this understanding to avoid bad behavior. Perhaps psychopaths know the difference between right and wrong and they just don't care about it. Nichols (2002) explores a possibility along these lines, as do Fischer and Ravizza (1998: 76–81). From this perspective it might not be clear that there is any problem with holding psychopaths responsible for their behavior, and some – Glannon (1997), Greenspan (2003), Maibom (2008), Shoemaker (2014), and Vargas and Nichols (2007) – have argued that the psychopath's partial capacity for distinguishing between right and wrong is sufficient for a degree of moral (or perhaps merely legal) responsibility.

However, even if we allow that psychopaths lack proper moral motivation and that they can in some sense grasp that their actions are wrong, there is still reason to worry that their capacity for moral understanding is too superficial to support true moral blameworthiness. This is because psychopaths seem to lack what R. Jay Wallace calls a "participant understanding" of moral discourse and moral reasoning (1996: 178): psychopaths don't engage with moral language and moral reasons in the way that members of the moral community do, and in an important sense our moral practices are alien to them. As Gary Watson puts it,

> Psychopaths appear to know what morality "requires" of them in the same way that they know that one must pay

income taxes and that smoking in commercial airplanes is against the rules. What they cannot understand is that those requirements have any kind of nonstrategic normative force for anyone; that is, they cannot regard moral demands as anything more than coercive pressures. They can know that what they aim to do might hurt someone, but not that there is any sort of (noninstrumental) reason against doing or having done it. (2011: 309)

So, while psychopaths can in a way recognize what morality requires, they lack the capacity "to comprehend moral demands as normatively relevant"; thus, moral considerations cannot bear (except perhaps indirectly) on their decision-making and, as Watson notes, "this is a significant impairment of practical thought" (ibid.). Perhaps it is a significant enough impairment to call into question the psychopath's moral responsibility.

Psychopathy and Contempt

It's important to keep in mind how different the psychopath is from a slave-owner like Scarlet who – despite believing that slavery is permissible – should be thought of as a relatively normal person. We should imagine, for example, that Scarlet has a participant's understanding of moral discourse, that she has moral respect for (at least some) other people, and that she is not markedly impaired for feeling empathy toward (at least some) other people. Of course, we stipulated that, given her social context, it's not reasonable to expect Scarlet to recognize her slaves' moral standing. But, since this failure of moral insight occurs against the backdrop of her recognition of the moral standing of non-slaves, it is plausible to characterize Scarlet as denying that her slaves have this standing. And insofar as her treatment of her slaves expresses this conviction, her treatment of them seems straightforwardly contemptuous.

But now consider a psychopath – let's call him Ted. Since Ted does not have a participant's understanding of moral discourse, he cannot deploy concepts such as "moral standing" in the way that Scarlet does, and it is therefore much less straightforward to interpret Ted's actions as expressing the claim that other people lack moral standing. But, if this is right, it's not clear that Ted's behavior toward other people expresses morally relevant contempt for them even when he treats them quite badly. This would, in turn, seem to call his moral blameworthiness into question (at least for accounts of blameworthiness in which contempt and ill will play a central role).

Neil Levy defends this perspective on psychopaths when he claims that contempt (of the sort relevant to blameworthiness) is a "moralized attitude" and that only moral agents who are "capable of appreciating moral facts" can express such contempt through their behavior (2007: 135). For Levy, an expression of moral contempt requires more than a failure to adhere to moral norms, it requires the *rejection* or *flouting* of such norms, and on Levy's view this can be accomplished only by someone who grasps the significance of moral norms in a way that the psychopath cannot (ibid.; Levy follows Watson [1987] 2004a on this point). Similarly, David Shoemaker argues that, while a psychopath like Ted certainly fails to express respect for other people, he is incapable of expressing the sort of blame-grounding *disrespect* that would make resentment appropriate because such disrespect requires a kind of moral sense that he lacks (2011: 629).[9]

On views like those of Levy and Shoemaker, the psychopath is blameless in the way that a normal person would be blameless if she did something wrong without having had any way of seeing that her behavior was wrong. Here is an example from Levy that is meant to illustrate this point:

> Suppose there is a kind of harm that is objectively morally relevant, but of which we are ignorant. Suppose, for instance, that plants can be harmed, and that this harm is a moral reason against killing or treading on them. In that case, many of us are (causally) responsible for a great many moral harms. But it is false that we express contempt, ill-will, or even *moral* indifference to these plants. Nor do we *flout* their standing as objects to whom moral consideration is owed. These attitudes all require a background of normative beliefs for their expression, in the relevant sense. Absence of moral regard does not entail, indeed it is incompatible with, presence of moral disregard. But just as we fail to express any moral attitudes

toward plants, so psychopaths fail to express the relevant attitudes toward their victims. (2007: 135)

David Shoemaker (2011: 625) makes use of a similar, though more complex, example, and Gary Watson (2002: 240) also uses a related example to make a similar point. I reply to Shoemaker's example in detail in Talbert (2012b).

Certainly the people in Levy's example do not express the kind of contempt or ill will for plants that could ground moral blame. Note, however, that we can explain this by referencing the fact that they are unaware of the consequences of their actions – they are unaware, for example, that uprooting a plant causes it pain (or whatever it is that is supposed to be the morally relevant harm done to the plant). But psychopaths are often in quite a different position: they may well know that they harm others. What they are incapable of understanding is that this gives them a non-instrumental reason to refrain from certain behaviors.

Because a psychopath cannot deploy moral concepts, we cannot attribute to him the kinds of judgments that someone like Scarlet can make: a judgment such as, "You don't have moral standing, so I can treat you how I like." However, in a case in which a psychopath is aware of the likely consequences of his action, it does seem reasonable to attribute to him a judgment such as, "The fact that my action will hurt you is no reason to refrain from it" or, even worse, a judgment such as, "The fact that my action will hurt is *a reason* to do it." These latter judgments, of which at least some psychopaths are apparently capable, issue from a perspective according to which the suffering of other people can be overlooked, and we might think that such judgments (and the actions to which they give rise) are plausibly thought of as contemptuous and thus as meriting moral blame.

Perhaps, then, all that's required for an agent to be an appropriate target of blame is that he possesses very general powers of rationality and self-government – for example, the ability to count something as a reason for acting and to act on that basis. This might be enough for an agent to express contempt and ill will (or closely related attitudes) through his behavior. T. M. Scanlon makes a proposal along these lines (though he doesn't mention psychopaths specifically). As

Scanlon notes, "[i]f a creature cannot make judgments about reasons at all, then its actions...cannot reflect judgment-sensitive attitudes of the kind that challenge our moral standing and make resentment an appropriate reaction" (1998: 288). However, "a rational creature who fails to see the force of moral reasons...can nonetheless understand that a given action will injure others and can judge that this constitutes no reason against so acting" (ibid.). Scanlon concludes that "the actions of such a creature would have implications for its relations with others that are at least very similar to (if not identical with) those of" a normal, morally competent wrongdoer (ibid.).

Part of Scanlon's point, I take it, is that a judgment such as, "The fact that my action will hurt you isn't a reason to refrain," can have interpersonal meaning for us, or what we might call moral significance, even though it is not a judgment with explicit moral content. Note, for example, that this judgment is entirely opposed to our own thinking about the significance our suffering ought to have for an agent who, like the psychopath, is in the business of making judgments about reasons. From our own point of view, the judgment in question involves a serious moral error and is not one that would be made by a person of good will. So perhaps this sort of judgment, of which the psychopath is apparently capable, is enough for blameworthiness (Talbert 2008, 2014).

On the other hand, if the rational impairments of some actual psychopaths are much broader than what I have indicated here, they will be less suited for responsibility on the model I have described. See Greenspan (2003), Fine and Kennett (2004), and Litton (2010) for accounts that emphasize the possibility of broader rational impairments on the part of psychopaths.

4.3   The Conversational Model of Moral Responsibility

A number of philosophers have recently emphasized the conversational aspects of our moral responsibility practices. Moral blame, in particular, seems to be largely a means of getting a point across, of expressing our moral values and our condemnation of those whose behavior conflicts with these values. More generally, it may be illuminating to think of the give-and-take involved in holding responsible, apologizing, and forgiving as analogous to moves made in a conversation.

Conversational models of moral responsibility typically accept some form of moral competence requirement. It's easy to see why: if we believe that blame is an attempt at moral communication, then it is natural to regard blame as appropriate only in the case of morally competent agents who can be reached by our communicative efforts. Gary Watson defends a version of this position when he argues that the "negative reactive attitudes" involved in blame "express a *moral* demand, a demand for reasonable regard" and that, "[t]o be intelligible, demanding presumes understanding on the part of the object of the demand" ([1987] 2004a: 229–30). Watson concludes that, if our moral demands are not intelligible to an agent because he lacks moral competence, he is not a fit target for blaming responses that express these demands.

One concern we might have about Watson's position is that it involves a mainly instrumental or forward-looking account of blame, as if the point of blame were simply to bring about certain results: a successful communicative act, moral recognition on the part of a wrongdoer, and so forth. Perhaps this goal-oriented focus risks losing sight of the degree to which blame is concerned with the past and with wrongful acts already committed. A related worry about the conversational model is that it seems perfectly reasonable to blame people even in cases in which our conversational goals cannot be achieved, as when we blame the dead or others who will never be aware of, and cannot respond to, the fact that we blame them.

On inspection, neither of these objections seems very promising (though I shall return to both in different forms at the end of this chapter). As for the first objection, while there is certainly a forward-looking component to the conversational model of responsibility, the approach can't plausibly be accused of ignoring the past. On a view like Watson's, blame is explicitly a response to the moral status of past actions; it's just that Watson takes our responses to these actions to be constrained by norms of intelligibility.

The second objection also misfires: there is no problem with blaming the dead because nothing in the conversational model requires that blame must be successfully communicated to the one who is blamed. As R. Jay Wallace explains (in defending a view similar to Watson's), membership in the community of morally responsible agents depends on a moral relationship that is

> defined by the successful exchange of moral criticism and justification. This is not to say that in holding people responsible we are always engaged in such an exchange – clearly we can hold people accountable even if we do not communicate with them at all, and even if we have no interest in literally exchanging criticism and justification with them. But it will be reasonable to hold accountable only someone who is at least a candidate for this kind of exchange of criticism and justification...the stance of holding people accountable involves a susceptibility to sanctioning behavior whose function is essentially to express the reactive emotions. Insofar as these responses are bound up with the moral obligations we accept, they will only be fully intelligible as forms of expression when addressed to people who are capable of grasping moral reasons. (1996: 164)

So what's required is not that blame is actually communicated to a wrongdoer, or that the wrongdoer responds appropriately to this communication, but that the wrongdoer is (or at least was, if he is deceased) a candidate for this sort of communicative endeavor.

Michael McKenna takes a similar approach in his recent book *Conversation and Responsibility* (2012). McKenna notes that blaming the dead is just one instance of the many cases in which blame occurs in the absence of the blamed, and he argues that all of these cases should be "understood in terms of how the one who blames would respond to, and...converse with, the one blamed were the blamer in the presence of the blamed" (2012: 177). McKenna's book is the most focused and detailed presentation of the conversational model of moral responsibility available. On his view, a "moral responsibility exchange" takes place in stages. The first stage is the initial "moral contribution" of an actor (using McKenna's example: suppose that Leslie tells a racist joke); next, there is a stage of "moral address" (Daphne responds to Leslie with moral blame because of the joke); this may be followed by a stage of "moral account" (Leslie might acknowledge the offense she caused and ask for Daphne's forgiveness); other stages in this moral "conversation" can build on these three initial steps (ibid.: 89).

Note that, whereas authors such as Watson and Wallace focus on the expressive aspect of blaming responses, McKenna's account begins with the moral (and conversational) significance of the action for which an agent is blamed. For him, a guilty action is the first move in a moral conversation, and this is one reason why moral competence is required for moral responsibility. McKenna gives an expansive account of this competence: it involves not just the ability to recognize the moral demands that a person expresses in her blame of you but also your own ability to hold other people morally responsible. Similar to the way in which a "linguistically competent agent" must be able not only to express herself but also "to interpret others effectively, a morally responsible agent's ability to be morally responsible... is dependent upon her ability to hold [others] morally responsible" (McKenna 2012: 88). An agent who lacks this ability cannot, on McKenna's view, engage with us in a way that could count as the first move in a moral conversation:

> The agent who is incapable of participating in the complex social practices through which her reactive attitudes can be expressed is...impaired in her ability both to appreciate the challenges put to her by those who hold morally responsible, and to hold others morally responsible by likewise challenging them; she is also handicapped in her ability to be morally responsible...*She is impaired in such a way that she is incapable of acting from a will with a moral quality that could be a candidate for assessment from the standpoint of holding responsible.* (ibid.: 78, emphasis added)

For McKenna, then, severely morally impaired agents are not candidates for blame not just because they cannot be reached by moral communication, but also because they lack the tools to initiate a genuine moral conversation in the first place. The point here is perhaps similar to the one we saw Levy and Shoemaker defend above regarding the psychopath's inability to express genuine moral contempt or ill will through his behavior.

Conversation, Psychopaths, and Merely Incorrigible Wrongdoers

So how would the conversational model of responsibility deal with someone like Scarlet the slave-owner who, as I described her above, finds it very difficult – if not impossible – to recognize the significance of certain moral considerations and yet is not globally incapacitated for responsiveness to moral reasons? Gary Watson argues, in the paper of his that I cited a few paragraphs above, that blaming attitudes such as resentment "are incipiently forms of communication, which makes sense only on the assumption that the other can comprehend the message" and that, "[i]n a certain sense, blaming and praising those with diminished moral understanding loses its 'point'" ([1987] 2004a: 230). We might take this to suggest that Scarlet is not an appropriate target for robust blaming responses such as resentment since we can't reasonably expect her to engage with our moral communication – our blame – in the desired way: she's so committed to her racist views that she almost certainly won't be persuaded to rethink her views about slavery or about the moral status of slaves.

Some might be attracted to an argument like the preceding, but it doesn't seem to match Watson's considered view on the subject. In a recent paper, Watson draws a contrast between incorrigible wrongdoers like Scarlet (Watson mentions Nazis, Mafiosos, and white supremacists) and psychopaths (2011: 318). Watson says that merely incorrigible wrongdoers, unlike psychopaths, can sometimes make "a genuine return to the moral point of view" because they possess "suppressed or partial or partitioned moral sensibilities that are somehow reengaged or extended" (ibid.). Perhaps the possibility of a "return" to morality is enough to make Scarlet a candidate for the moral communication involved in blame. And even if we know that Scarlet will never return to the moral point of view – and even if she never inhabited that point of view in the first place – the fact that she has at least a partial sense of morality would seem to legitimize attempts at moral communication in her case. Scarlet's partial moral sense means that she has a participant's understanding of our moral demands: she knows what we are doing when we put moral demands to her – she simply rejects them. The status of psychopaths, however, is quite different.

In contrast to Neil Levy and David Shoemaker, Watson allows that psychopaths are capable of morally significant bad behavior. For Watson, since "[p]sychopaths are capable of a complex mode of reflective agency," their behavior "is ethically significant in ways that the activities of less complex creatures cannot be": they are, for example, "not just dangerous but cruel" and capable of being invested in their bad behavior in a way that "constitutes...malice" (2011: 316). Thus, "[w]e rightly predicate viciousness of the attitudes and conduct of psychopaths" and, for Watson, attributing viciousness and malice to psychopaths amounts to holding them morally responsible in a limited way (ibid.: 308). (Here Watson invokes the distinction between responsibility-as-attributability and responsibility-as-accountability described in §2.4.)

However, on Watson's view (and on the views of other advocates of the conversational model), psychopaths are not open to moral blame in the more serious sense of being properly targeted with negative attitudes such as resentment. This is because psychopaths "lack the capacity for moral reciprocity or mutual recognition that is necessary for intelligibly holding someone accountable to basic moral demands and expectations" (2011: 308). As Watson sees things, "what is a proper object of moral horror and hard feelings [i.e., the psychopath's behavior] does not necessarily warrant resentment and indignation"; thus, in the case of the psychopath, "[t]hese latter responses must fall short of their erstwhile targets" (ibid.: 317). Resentment and related attitudes fall short in the case of the psychopath because these attitudes commit us "to the appropriateness of [taking up] an inherently communicative stance" toward the one whom we target with these responses (ibid.: 328 n.35). In sum, since resentment presumes that its target is an apt candidate for moral communication, dialogue, and rapprochement, it is not appropriate with respect to psychopaths.

Of course, we would reach a very different conclusion from Watson's about the blameworthiness of psychopaths if we focused more narrowly on the way that blame and resentment respond to the moral quality of past actions and to the quality of will that informed those actions. (Here I return both to the first objection to Watson mentioned at the beginning of this section and to the account of resentment presented in my response to the Fairness Argument in §4.1.) An approach that adopted this narrow focus might allow for serious, resentment-involving blame even in the absence of moral competence, as long as it is possible for an agent who lacks moral competence to express morally significant contempt and ill will through her behavior. Moreover, this alternative approach need not deny that moral blame is often an attempt at moral communication or that blame performs a valuable function when it leads to fruitful moral exchanges. All the account under consideration must insist on is that, while blame *can* achieve these communicative ends, the prospect of its doing so is not necessary for legitimizing an instance of blame. Indeed, the apparent legitimacy of blaming the dead highlights the way in which blame can be apt even when it cannot plausibly aim at initiating moral dialogue.

But what would be the point of blame, and of attitudes such as resentment, in the case of globally morally impaired agents? Since the psychopath cannot conform to the moral demands that we express through our blame, we should *not* understand blame in the psychopath's case as primarily issuing such demands. Instead, resentment and related blaming attitudes can be interpreted as ways of marking or acknowledging that one has been treated with contempt or ill will. Or, instead of offering an alternative theory of resentment, it may be that there are multiple resentment-like emotions that can play a role in blame. Perhaps there is a resentment-like attitude that is characterized by the thought that the one who wronged us is a potential partner in moral conversation. This attitude would certainly presume a capacity for moral dialogue, but there might be closely related blaming emotions characterized merely by the thought that another has wronged us or has treated us with contempt or with an illegitimate lack of concern.

This second form of resentment could be interpreted not as expressing a demand for conformity with a moral norm but simply as noting and protesting a violation of that norm. One could stand up for a moral principle in this way – e.g., the principle that you have a sort of standing that makes it wrong to disregard the normative status of your welfare – without having any expectation that the blamed party will, or could, appreciate the moral principle for which one is standing up. In a way, this is a communicative act, but it is not one that presumes moral sense on the part of the blamed.

On the sort of view just elaborated, we might admit both that psychopaths are not part of our moral community in the sense of being potential partners in a moral conversation and that this makes them inappropriate targets for specific blaming responses (e.g., those responses that are sensible only when directed at potential moral conversationalists). However, psychopaths may still be members of our moral community in a significant way since they can wrong us (as opposed to merely injuring us), and this may be enough to justify blaming them in the strong sense that involves negative reactive attitudes such as (some version of) resentment (Talbert 2014).

4.4 Conclusion

The previous chapter focused on the personal and causal histories of agents, and this issue has come up again in this chapter, though in a different way. The concern here has been not just with how a person's dispositions and values are shaped by factors outside her control but also with the ways these factors can impair the person's ability to respond to moral reasons.

We encountered, once again, the conflict between austere approaches to responsibility that focus on the moral quality of behavior and the current control agents exercise over their behavior and, on the other hand, approaches that take there to be additional conditions on moral responsibility, such as the moral competence requirement. I tried to explain how the austere, attributionist approach might be applied both to locally and to globally morally impaired agents. As I noted, this application is more straightforward in the case of locally impaired agents, since it is clearer that we can attribute objectionable moral judgments to these agents. Some proponents of the moral competence condition (such as Levy and Shoemaker) have argued that, if an agent lacks this competence, her behavior will also fail to have the moral properties to which blame responds. Others (like Watson) have argued that, while a severely morally impaired wrongdoer's behavior can have blame-relevant moral qualities, blame may still be inappropriate because there are norms of intelligibility – or what we might call conversational norms – that also apply to blame. Finally, McKenna's conversational model of responsibility appears to combine both of the preceding perspectives.

The next chapter focuses on the kinds of knowledge or awareness that are required for moral responsibility. Some themes from this chapter will be relevant to that discussion, since we might think that a significant (and perhaps responsibility-undermining) moral impairment is present when an agent is, in one way or another, prevented from acquiring certain forms of knowledge, such as knowledge of the moral status of her behavior.

4.5   Further Reading

In §4.1, I suggested that blame is a way of taking seriously the wrong done to a victim. Several recent works have explored the link between blame and taking wrongs seriously: Bennett (2013), Franklin (2013), Sher (2006), Wallace (2013). The first really influential treatment of psychopathy is Hervey Cleckley's book *The Mask of Sanity* ([1941] 1976). A more up-to-date introduction to the subject can be found in Robert Hare's *Without Conscience* (1993). Hare is the author of the widely used diagnostic tool mentioned in §4.2, and his book describes the basics of his diagnostic approach. In *The Psychopath* (2005), James Blair and his colleagues lay out the basics of their compelling neuro-cognitive account of the genetic and environmental origins of psychopathy. Two anthologies with essays on the responsibility status of psychopaths are Malatesti and McMillan (2010) and Schramme (2014). For more on the contrast between psychopaths and merely incorrigible wrongdoers, see Nelkin (2015). One important defense of the moral competence requirement that I have not discussed is found in Stephen Darwall's *The Second-Person Standpoint* (2006), which includes important elements of the conversational model of responsibility. Indeed, McKenna cites Darwall's work, along with that of Watson ([1987] 2004a) and of Russell (2004), as an influence; he also notes that Lucas (1993), Oshana (2004), and Pettit (2001) advance earlier conversational or "discursive" accounts of responsibility (McKenna 2012: 88 n.7). At the end of this chapter, I considered the possibility that blame might be construed as expressing a moral protest rather than a moral demand. For interpretations of blame as a form of moral protest, see Hieronymi (2001), Smith (2013), and Talbert (2012a). For an account that calls into question the idea that blame is best interpreted as expressing demands, see Macnamara (2013).

5

The Epistemic Dimension of Responsibility

It is fairly common to distinguish between two conditions on moral responsibility: a control condition and an epistemic condition, or what we might call a freedom condition and a knowledge condition. A control condition specifies the type or degree of control an agent must have over her behavior in order to be morally responsible for it. Epistemic conditions, on the other hand, focus on the kind of awareness that is required for moral responsibility: for example, awareness of the likely consequences of one's actions or perhaps of their moral status. Something like this distinction goes all the way back to Aristotle's observation, in Book III of *Nicomachean Ethics*, that an action is involuntary (and hence blameless) either when an agent is forced to act as she does or when she is in some significant way ignorant of the action that she performs (1999: 30 [1110a]).[10]

While a distinction between control and epistemic conditions has often been employed, until quite recently it was the former condition that received almost all the attention. This was because so much work on moral responsibility was concerned with free will and, particularly, with the question of whether determinism interferes with the kind of control required for free will and moral responsibility. However, since this book is not concerned primarily with the problem of determinism, it is not surprising that we have already encountered issues relevant to the epistemic dimension of moral responsibility. For example, we saw in chapter 2 that, according to advocates of attributionism, agents may be morally responsible for actions that they perform inadvertently – all that is required is that the behavior in question is attributable to the agent in a way that opens her up to moral assessment. Reference to moral knowledge also played an important role in the previous chapter's discussion of moral competence: as several authors have argued, one way in which moral competence can be undermined is through the inculcation of false moral beliefs.

It is easy to think of cases in which ignorance excuses. To adapt an example from the last chapter, suppose that it turns out that plants feel pain when they are uprooted. Now, even if this were true, there is little evidence in favor of this supposition. Therefore, most of us don't believe that plants feel pain, so we don't know that plants feel pain, and this lack of knowledge would be perfectly reasonable even if it turned out that plants *do* feel pain. So, even if plants do feel pain, the fact that we are unaware that they do – and that it is reasonable for us to be unaware – insulates us from blame for causing them pain. More prosaic cases abound: if I am not aware that an action of mine will injure you and I have no reason to think that my action will have that effect, then in most cases I would not be blameworthy for injuring you by performing the action. In such a case there is nothing for your blame to latch onto, since nothing about my action indicates the sort of contempt or unconcern to which blame responds.

On the other hand, it's also clear that ignorance does not always excuse. Consider the facts of a 1929 case from the US state of Oregon (*State v. Newberg et al.*). Two men, Newberg and Black, were hunting deer at night (which was illegal) not too far from a road. They took turns firing at what they supposed to be a deer, each assisting and encouraging the other as he fired. Upon approaching their quarry, Newberg and Black discovered that they had just killed a man and his horse. From a legal standpoint, the interesting question here is how to apportion liability, given that the defendants acted in concert but it was impossible to tell which of the two fired the fatal shot. What is of relatively little interest is the question of whether the defendants' ignorance of what they were doing exonerated them – it seems obvious that it did not. Of course, the fact that Newberg and Black did not know that they were shooting at a person means that they were not guilty of certain crimes (murder, for example, is often defined as involving "malice aforethought" or premeditation). But, even so, they are clearly not generally exonerated (either morally or legally) by their ignorance in the way that a person would be if she accidently fired a gun while suffering a seizure.

A natural way of explaining the legal and moral culpability of the two men is to say that they *should have known* what they were doing. More precisely, it should have occurred to them that there was a good chance that it was not a deer at which they were shooting, and this uncertainty should have led them to hold their fire. Moreover, Newberg and Black shouldn't have been hunting at night (and near a road) because this is just the sort of thing that will make it difficult to tell whether you are shooting at a deer or a man on a horse. Our sense that, to some significant degree, Newberg and Black are blameworthy presumably hangs on considerations such as these.

We'll get deeper into these issues throughout the rest of this chapter. I'll begin by considering an argument for skepticism about moral responsibility that is based on epistemic considerations. This discussion of skepticism will make implicit reference to the topic of *tracing*, and in the second half of the chapter I'll focus explicitly on the use of tracing in theories of moral responsibility. We employ tracing when we declare that, even if a person did not meet the control or knowledge conditions on moral responsibility at the time of action, she may still be morally responsible if we can causally trace her action back to a choice she made when she did satisfy these conditions.

5.1   Unwitting Wrongdoing and Skepticism about Moral Responsibility

In her important essay "Culpable Ignorance," Holly Smith argues that, if an agent's ignorance is culpable – as it is in many of the cases in which we say things such as "he should

have known better" – the agent must have performed a
benighting act – an act "in which the agent fails to improve
(or positively impairs) his cognitive position" and in virtue
of which he subsequently performs an "unwitting wrongful
act" (1983: 547). The basic idea is that, if you are blameworthy for your ignorance, the ignorance must in some way be
your fault. Here are two examples of benighting acts from
Smith: a doctor fails to read a particular medical journal and
so does not know how best to treat a patient; a near-sighted
person drives off without her glasses and injures a child on
the road because she did not see him (ibid.: 544–5). Newberg
and Black's decision to hunt at night similarly contributes to
their poor epistemic position and subsequent wrongdoing.

Of course, for ignorance to be culpable it is not enough
that it arises from a benighting act. Presumably, the ignorant
agent must also be culpable for the benighting act itself, for,
"[i]f the agent had an excuse for the benighting act, then the
subsequent wrongful act is obviously blameless as well"
(Smith 1983: 548). There might, for example, be a very good
reason why the near-sighted driver left without her glasses or
the doctor did not read the medical journal, and, if we would
not blame these agents for their benighting acts, we also
should not blame them for the subsequent harms that followed from their ignorance.

This raises a question: How exactly do we come to be
blameworthy for our benighting acts? One proposal, pursued
separately by Gideon Rosen (2003, 2004, 2008) and Michael
Zimmerman (1997, 2008), is that we are blameworthy for
our benighting acts only to the degree that we knowingly and
willingly engaged in these actions. The basic idea here is that,
if ignorance excuses, the ultimate source of blame for an
action done in ignorance must be an instance of knowing
wrongdoing. Put the other way around, if a wrong done in
ignorance has its source merely in other actions done in ignorance, there are no grounds for blame.

Consider the following example from Gideon Rosen:

> Suppose a surgeon orders that her type A patient be trans-
> fused with type B blood, that she does this only because she
> is mistaken about the patient's blood type, and that she is
> mistaken about the blood type only because she neglected to

double-check his chart (which had just been updated) immediately prior to surgery, as standard practice requires. Then
we know this much. The surgeon is culpable [i.e., blamewor-
thy] for the bad transfusion (and the ensuing harm) only if
she is culpable for her ignorance as to the patient's blood type,
and she is culpable for her ignorance only if she is culpable
for her negligent failure to double-check the chart. Now focus
on *this* negligent failure... It is plausible that in this case, as
in most similar cases, the negligent failure will itself be an act
done from ignorance. When the time is ripe for precaution,
the agent will fail to take it only because she does not then
think – and so does not then *know* – that she ought to be
taking it. But if the failure is thoughtless in this sense... the
agent will be culpable for it only if she is culpable for the
ignorance that underlies it... she will be culpable for *this* bit
of ignorance only if she is culpable for omitting some required
precaution to prevent *it* – e.g., if she is forgetful, asking one
of her colleagues to remind her to check the chart. (2004: 303)

So, on Rosen's view, the surgeon will be culpable for mistakenly harming her patient only if she is culpable for failing
to do the thing that prevented her from knowing that her
action was harmful. Now suppose, as Rosen suggests, that
the surgeon's benighting act – really a benighting omission
– is that she didn't ask someone to remind her to double-
check her patient's blood type. Rosen's point is that this
omission will ground blameworthiness only if the surgeon
is culpable for it, and Rosen believes that the surgeon is
culpable for the omission only if it was done knowingly.
Therefore, what would be required for the surgeon to be
blameworthy is something like the following: she thinks to
herself, "I'm forgetful, so I really ought to ask someone to
remind me to double-check my patient's blood type," and
then, thinking that this is what she ought to do, the surgeon
doesn't do it.

Thus, for Rosen, ignorance is culpable only if it has its
origin in an instance of *akrasia* or weakness of will – that is,
an instance in which an agent clearly knows what she ought
to do and nonetheless fails to do it. On Rosen's view, since
ignorance tends to excuse, "responsibility for action done
from ignorance is invariably a matter of derivative responsibility," which is to say that "[o]ne is responsible for the act

done from ignorance only if one is independently responsible for something else" (2004: 307). But this means that the ultimate or original source of responsibility for an action done in ignorance cannot be another action done in ignorance, which "entails that *the only possible locus of original responsibility is an akratic act*...a knowing sin" (ibid., emphasis in original). Michael Zimmerman has a closely related view:

> If one is culpable for nonignorant behavior, then, of course, one's culpability involves a lack of ignorance. If, in contrast, one is culpable for ignorant behavior, then one is culpable for the ignorance to which this behavior may be traced...But one is never in direct control of whether one is ignorant...Indirect culpability for something presupposes direct culpability for something else. Whatever this something else is, it cannot be ignorant behavior, because then the argument would apply all over again to this behavior. Hence all culpability can be traced to culpability that involves lack of ignorance, that is, that involves a belief on the agent's part that he or she is doing something morally wrong. (1997: 418)

Rosen and Zimmerman apply the above reasoning not just to cases in which an agent is ignorant about the context in which she acts – as with the surgeon who does not know that she is transfusing a type A patient – but also to cases in which an agent is ignorant of moral truths. In this vein, Rosen offers the case of an "ambitious capitalist who is mistaken about where to draw the line between permissibly aggressive business practice and reprehensibly ruthless business practice" (2004: 305). This capitalist

> knows that if he outsources the accounting department, he will expose a significant number of loyal employees to profound hardship; but he also knows that the move will improve the bottom line; that his shareholders have certain legitimate expectations, etc. Suppose that as a matter of fact the marginal improvement in the bottom line does not justify the profound harm to his employees, but that our capitalist, after considering the question, fails to see this. (Ibid.)

Note that, while Rosen's capitalist reaches the wrong conclusion about how to behave, it's possible that he never engaged in knowing wrongdoing and never managed his moral opinions in a way that he regarded as deficient. "It is not hard to imagine," says Rosen, that "our capitalist does something seriously wrong without knowing that he is doing something wrong," that he "knows all the relevant non-normative facts" about the circumstances in which he acts, and that "he has been adequately reflective, careful, etc.," in thinking about how he ought to behave (2004: 305).

Rosen's account of this case may sound strange, since the capitalist's reflection clearly wasn't careful enough to allow him to discover how he actually ought to behave. However, it's plausible to assume that people can sometimes be as reflective and careful as can reasonably be expected, but that they wind up reaching the wrong conclusion all the same. Perhaps, as Rosen suggests, "the people who taught [the capitalist] how to think about such cases taught him badly. Perhaps it's just a hard case and after thinking about it for a decent interval he has simply arrived at the wrong answer" (2004: 305). At any rate, Rosen argues that, if you accept the claim that the capitalist always managed his moral opinions in the way he sincerely thought best, "you will find it plausible that his moral ignorance is not his fault" and, if you accept this second claim, you should "find it equally compelling that it would be a mistake to blame him for the wrong he does" (ibid.).

The same point is meant to apply to more serious – and, from our perspective, more obvious – instances of wrongdoing. For example, Rosen says that a "slaveholder who... believes that [slavery] is morally permissible" will be blameworthy "only if he is culpable for the moral ignorance from which he acts" (2004: 304). And we might think – on the basis of the kinds of considerations introduced in Scarlet's case in the last chapter (§4.1) – that at least some slaveholders were not culpable for their moral ignorance (cf. Rosen 2003: 64–5).

So how does all this lead to skepticism about moral responsibility? For one thing, Rosen argues that, insofar as moral responsibility requires knowing wrongdoing, we shouldn't place *"much confidence in any particular positive judgment of responsibility,"* since we are rarely in a position to know that a person has exhibited the relevant sort of weakness of will (2004: 308, emphasis in original). Moreover, and as William FitzPatrick points out (2008: 599), even if we are more confident than Rosen in our ability accurately to attribute weakness of will to other people, it is possible that a great many normal wrongdoers are not open to moral blame because there is no relevant instance of knowing wrongdoing in their past. In other words, perhaps very many wrongdoers are like Rosen's capitalist: they don't know that they are doing wrong and it is not their fault that they lack this knowledge.

Michael Zimmerman endorses a conclusion along these lines when he writes that people who exhibit "such moral vices as racism, sexism, and the like" are frequently "oblivious to the wrongness involved in their doing so," and therefore "responsibility for these vices and the vicious behavior in which they issue is incurred less frequently, perhaps far less frequently, than is commonly supposed" (1997: 425). Neil Levy also endorses a skeptical conclusion on epistemic grounds, arguing that "[t]he epistemic conditions" on moral responsibility "are so demanding that they are rarely satisfied" and that, in cases of unwitting wrongdoing, there often "is no plausible candidate for a [culpable] benighting action" that could ground blameworthiness (2011b: 131).

5.2 Two Responses to the Skeptical Challenge

Let's agree for the moment that it would be unfair to blame someone like Rosen's ambitious capitalist for his ignorant wrongdoing if he were not also to blame for his moral ignorance. As we have seen, Rosen and Zimmerman believe that the capitalist would be blameworthy for his ignorance only if it could be traced back to an instance of knowing wrongdoing. However, an alternative view is that the capitalist is blameworthy for his moral ignorance (and his subsequent wrong actions) regardless of whether he engaged in knowing wrongdoing as long as it was reasonable to expect him to have taken steps to avoid, or to correct, the ignorance in question. William FitzPatrick offers a view along these lines.

Inspired by Rosen's capitalist, FitzPatrick considers the case of Mr Potter, the greedy and callous landlord who is the central villain in Frank Capra's 1946 film *It's a Wonderful Life*. Potter does many bad things in the movie, but let's assume that he subjects his moral values to what he regards as sufficient scrutiny and that he never acts contrary to these values. FitzPatrick notes that, even granting these assumptions, Mr Potter presumably has the general capacities required for recognizing that much of his behavior is not morally permissible; moreover, nothing about Potter's upbringing or social context would have made such recognition *impossible* for him (FitzPatrick 2008: 605). Indeed, an educated person like Mr Potter would have known that many other people take themselves to have good reason to reject his moral views.

So why is Mr Potter morally ignorant? Why doesn't he engage in the kind of self-critical moral reflection that would allow him to recognize the true moral status of his behavior? FitzPatrick suggests that Potter's failure in this regard is most likely explained by "voluntary exercises of vices such as over-confidence, arrogance, dismissiveness, laziness, dogmaticism, incuriosity, self-indulgence, contempt, and so on" (2008: 605). These vices lead him to be excessively confident in his own moral position and summarily to reject views that call it into question. But, if this is what explains Potter's moral ignorance, FitzPatrick argues that his ignorance doesn't amount to an excuse. After all, isn't it reasonable to expect Potter not to be vicious and thus to have taken advantage of available opportunities to avoid or correct his moral ignorance? So, on FitzPatrick's view, Potter is blameworthy for the bad behavior that issues from his moral ignorance even if his moral ignorance is not the result of a prior akratic act.

At this point, however, a reply can be made on Rosen's and Zimmerman's behalf. Perhaps the very fact that Potter is vice-ridden in the way that FitzPatrick describes makes it unreasonable to expect him to engage sincerely with moral outlooks different from his own. As Neil Levy points out, given the degree to which Mr Potter's point of view is corrupted by his vices, "by his lights, Potter governs his normative views adequately" and "gives competing views the attention he takes them to deserve" (2009: 737). Potter is no doubt wrong in this judgment, but he thinks that he is behaving and deliberating just as he ought to.

It would seem that FitzPatrick has to allow this description of Potter's case since the point of his discussion is that Potter can be blameworthy even though he never engaged in knowing wrongdoing. But, with this assumption in hand, Levy argues, "if Potter does not see that he is managing his moral views badly, he has no (internal) reason to manage them any differently" (2009: 737). In other words, while Potter may be managing his moral views badly from the point of view of *objective* morality, given Potter's *subjective* moral values and beliefs (which, by hypothesis, he does not know are wrong), he may be governing himself in a perfectly rational and consistent way. This means that the expectation that Potter should manage his moral views differently amounts to asking him to behave in a way that is, from his subjective point of view, irrational. And Levy argues that this is an unfair expectation (ibid.: 739). If, by his own lights and with perfect internal consistency, Potter regards the moral criticism to which he is subjected as the "whining of socialists or sissies" (ibid.: 737), how can he be expected to take such criticism seriously? And, if this is not a reasonable expectation, Levy argues that Potter can't be expected to correct his moral ignorance, so he is not open to moral blame for acting on his false moral beliefs.

FitzPatrick might reply that the reasonableness of expecting Potter to subject his moral views to better scrutiny derives from the fact that it is reasonable to expect him *not* to have vices that conflict with this scrutiny. As FitzPatrick points out, a person's "character traits are not merely given [to that person] but are formed, reformed, and continuously shaped by our choices from the point of moral maturity onward" (2008: 608). So perhaps it is reasonable to expect Potter to behave better insofar as it is reasonable to expect him to have shaped a better character for himself.

Unfortunately, Levy's argument can just as easily be applied to Potter's character-shaping choices. Why did Potter make the character-shaping choices that led him to acquire the vices that FitzPatrick attributes to him? It can't be that when he made these choices he knew that he was making himself morally worse (for Potter is not a knowing wrongdoer), so it must be that he regarded his character-shaping choices (if he was even aware of making them) as permissible. Of course, Potter was mistaken about the moral permissibility of these choices, but why was he mistaken in this way? Perhaps in the end we must simply say that he was born with a disposition toward vice and toward making bad choices. Or perhaps we will say that, when Potter made his first bad choices, he did so without recognizing their moral status and that these initial choices made it difficult for him to discern the nature of subsequent bad choices. But in neither of these cases is it clear that we can reasonably expect Potter to have made different choices than the ones he made, nor do we uncover an obvious initial source of culpability to which his responsibility for his later choices can be traced.

A Different Response to the Skeptical Challenge

The New Attributionist perspective outlined in previous chapters offers a different way of arguing that Potter is blameworthy even if he never engaged in knowing wrongdoing. From this perspective, we can agree with FitzPatrick that Mr Potter is blameworthy because his present choices express his vices, and we can also agree with Levy that it may not be reasonable to expect Potter to have avoided his vices or to expect him to make better choices given that he has these vices. What allows the attributionist to adopt this position is that she rejects an assumption made by all the other participants in this debate: she rejects the claim that it is fair to blame Mr Potter for his ignorant wrongdoing *only if* he is at fault for his ignorance (I develop this approach and the discussion in the preceding sections in more detail in Talbert 2013).

The basic point that attributionism makes in this context is that, even if an agent is not at fault for acquiring her moral ignorance, it can still be reasonable to attribute blame-grounding contempt or disregard for others to her. Perhaps Mr Potter never acted wrongly or irrationally by his own lights but, when he cuts the salaries of his impoverished workers or forecloses on an orphanage, these decisions reflect judgments about how others may be treated. For the attributionist, to the degree that we regard these judgments as attributable to Potter and as grounding moral objections against him, we should also see them as licensing blaming responses that express these objections.

But what about Neil Levy's claim, which we saw above, that it would be unfair to blame Potter for doing wrong if he had no internal reasons for omitting his bad behavior? Levy's point is that, if choosing to do the right thing is subjectively irrational for Potter, we cannot expect him to do the right thing and we cannot blame him when he fails to do it. The attributionist rejects this reasoning because she does not interpret blame as necessarily expressing an expectation that a wrongdoer should have acted differently than he did.[11] Attributionism is concerned with why a person *actually* did what she did, not with whether it would have been rational for her to do something else (as I noted in the last chapter, in this respect, attributionism is related to Frankfurt-style compatibilism). Perhaps Potter would have to make subjectively irrational choices in order to revise his moral views, but this does nothing to call into question his control over his behavior when he acts badly or the moral quality of the judgments that inform his bad behavior. In such cases, he may be exercising perfect reflective control over how he acts: he may be acting just as he wants to act and may be doing so based on his deepest values and for reasons that appear to him to count decisively in favor of so acting. But all this is just to say that Potter's bad behavior is fully attributable to him, that it speaks for him and shows where he stands morally, and thus that it is proper grounds for holding him morally accountable (at least on the sort of view about moral responsibility that I advocate).

As we have seen in this chapter and in chapter 3, some views hold that a person must have played a particular sort of role in acquiring her moral faults in order to be blamed for having them. From the attributionist perspective, this sort of approach runs together causal and moral responsibility in an unhelpful way (I made a similar suggestion about Galen Strawson's position in chapter 3). Mr Potter may not have played the relevant causal role in acquiring his faults, but this is a separate issue from whether his behavior expresses his moral faults in a way that makes him an appropriate target of moral blame.

Of course, from the other side's perspective, the attributionist picture gets things badly wrong: for Rosen, Zimmerman, and Levy (as well as for several authors whose views were considered in chapter 3), blameworthiness depends not merely on the way an agent is at the time of action but also on whether the agent had an "inculpating history" – that is, a history that grounds her culpability (Rosen 2004: 309). And, as Zimmerman and Levy are particularly effective at pointing out, it may be that far fewer wrongdoers than we ordinarily suppose have this sort of history.

5.3　Tracing

In the 1959 spy thriller *North by Northwest*, a case of mistaken identity entangles Cary Grant's character, Roger Thornhill, in an international espionage plot. In one scene, Thornhill is captured by a group of spies who physically force him to consume a great deal of alcohol and then to get behind the wheel of a car. Thornhill's captors plan for him to drive off a cliff, but he manages to lead them on a drunken car chase that forces several other drivers off the road and ends in a wreck with a police car.

Is Thornhill blameworthy for drunk driving and for whatever injuries he caused to other motorists? Plausibly, he is not. But note that this has little to do with the fact that, since Thornhill was very drunk, he was not capable of avoiding an accident while he was driving. Imagine how poorly this excuse would fare in an average case of drunk driving: "Your Honor, I admit that I drove into the school bus, but at the time I was too drunk to avoid it." Instead, what gets Thornhill off the hook is that he did not willingly choose to drive or to impair his driving ability. The average drunk driver, on the other hand, is typically taken to be blameworthy because he is responsible for impairing himself. Such a driver may not be in a position to avoid an accident when he is impaired by drink, but at the time he chose to drink (or at least to have his *first* drink) he was sober.

The preceding illustrates a common element in reasoning about moral responsibility: namely, reliance on a *tracing principle*. Tracing principles help us explain how a person can be responsible for an action when, at the time of action, she lacked some element of control or knowledge that seems crucial for moral responsibility. We substantiate the claim of responsibility in such a case by tracing the agent's lack of control or knowledge back to decisions that were made when the agent's abilities (and/or knowledge) were not compromised. Thus, the drunk driver is morally responsible because the actions he takes while impaired can be traced back to unimpaired choices. Similarly, and as we saw above, a person may be responsible for an action done in ignorance if her ignorance can be traced back to knowing wrongdoing.

While it is common for accounts of responsibility to appeal to tracing, until recently there has been little direct and detailed attention given to the topic.

The Trouble With Tracing

Manuel Vargas (2005) argues that, in many cases, tracing does not do as good a job as we might hope at resolving puzzles about moral responsibility. To this end, he offers several cases in which (i) it seems that we must make use of tracing to explain why an agent is morally responsible, but (ii) there is no relevant past act or omission to which we can trace the agent's behavior in a way that satisfactorily grounds his present moral responsibility.

One of Vargas's cases features Jeff the Jerk, an unpleasant fellow who "is rude and inconsiderate about the feelings of others" (2005: 271). However, Jeff doesn't necessarily try to be a jerk, it just comes naturally to him. One day at work, Jeff's boss assigns him the job of firing several long-time employees, and Jeff performs this task in a characteristically and unreflectively "rude and insensitive fashion" (ibid.). Is Jeff blameworthy?

On the one hand, people like Jeff typically seem blameworthy. On the other hand, Jeff fails to satisfy a plausible knowledge condition on moral responsibility, since his rudeness and insensitivity are non-deliberative, arising as they do out of unreflective habits and traits. But perhaps his acquisition of these habits and traits can be traced back to deliberate self-forming choices that he made earlier in life. However, as Vargas points out, even if this were so, it might also be true that Jeff's self-forming choices where made "under conditions where [Jeff] could not have reasonably foreseen the later consequences of having that disposition, habit, or character trait" (2005: 275).

Suppose, for example, that many years earlier, in order to improve his social standing in high school, Jeff decided to emulate the popular boys around him who happened to be jerks. In this way Jeff might have "inculcated in himself all the behaviors and attitudes that we would perceive to be jerk-like" (Vargas 2005: 275) and, after a while, acting like a jerk would have become natural and unreflective for him. However, as Vargas points out, under this scenario it is very plausible that "at no point during the process of becoming a jerk…did Jeff even conceive that his plan for personal improvement would include in its outcomes that he would some day lay off employees in a despicable fashion" (ibid.: 276).

So not only does Jeff unreflectively act like a jerk in the present, the decision to which his jerkiness can be traced might not be one that he could reasonably have expected would lead to his subsequent objectionable behavior. Thus, the application of tracing in this case may not help us see how he is blameworthy. And note that the problematic features of Jeff's case plausibly apply to a great many other agents besides Jeff, for, in general, "much of our character and self-formation happens when we are young and when our ability to reasonably foresee the future is at its worst" (Vargas 2005: 277). This last point amplifies some of the concerns raised in chapter 3 about the historical requirements on moral responsibility: perhaps present responsibility requires not just that I played a substantial role in acquiring the traits that shape my current behavior but also that I knew how those traits would shape it.

In a reply to Vargas, John Martin Fischer and Neal Tognazzini agree that teenaged Jeff can't reasonably have been expected to know that emulating jerks in high school would lead him, many years later, to callously fire people. However,

Fischer and Tognazzini argue that it is surely "reasonable to expect Jeff's younger self to have known that becoming a jerk would in all probability lead him to perform jerky actions" later in life, and they claim that the reasonableness of this expectation is enough to ground his blameworthiness for his subsequent bad behavior (2009: 538). As they put it,

> When you choose to be a jerk, you can be held accountable for your subsequent specific acts of jerkiness – but you might not know in advance what they will be in all their particular glory! Similarly, when you choose to get drunk, you can be held accountable for your subsequent behavior, even though you presumably do not know what it will be in all its florid particularity. (Ibid.)

Fischer and Tognazzini note that Vargas anticipates roughly their objection to his view. In response, Vargas suggests that Jeff's case could be modified so that we don't think of him as deliberately choosing to become *a jerk* but imagine him instead to have acquired "the relevant [jerky] characteristics...while conceiving of them under a different guise (e.g., being 'cool'), while blind to the negative aspects of the acquired trait or characteristic" (2005: 277 n.12). In reply to this amended version of the view, Fischer and Tognazzini argue that it is irrelevant that Jeff was "simply seeking to be 'cool'" and that he was "oblivious to the dark side...of what he was doing" (2009: 538). While there may be *some* choices that a person can't be expected to recognize will lead to jerky behavior, Jeff's choice to emulate the cool kids – who are jerks, after all – is not one of them. It should have been easy to see what such a choice would lead to. Thus, Fischer and Tognazzini maintain that it is still the case that "Jeff should have expected" that his choices would "lead to his treating others poorly" and that the reasonableness of this expectation makes Jeff morally responsible for his adult behavior (ibid.: 539).

I am sympathetic with Vargas's concerns about tracing, so I'll end this section by saying some things in defense of his conclusion; the points I'll make also resonate with the perspective we saw Rosen and Zimmerman defend earlier in this chapter. The first thing to note is that, even if Jeff *should have* recognized the likely consequences of developing certain traits, it doesn't necessarily follow that he is blameworthy. More generally, the mere fact that someone should have been aware of something doesn't mean that he is blameworthy when he fails to notice it. It seems to me that blameworthiness in such a case also requires that the failure of awareness should reflect a blameworthy outlook on the agent's part: for example, disregard for the moral status of his choices and for the effects these choices will have on others. But, again, the mere fact that someone fails to notice or to be aware of something that he ought to have noticed does not necessarily mean that his concern for morality, or for the effects of his actions on others, is deficient in a way that grounds moral blame.

This last claim is supported, I think, by reflecting on cases in which we excuse a person for not noticing something that she ought to have noticed. We're all familiar with cases in which we fail to be as observant or reflective as we ought to be, or in which we fail to anticipate things that we ought to have anticipated. Occasionally, we can excuse ourselves in these cases by explaining why our attention was legitimately distracted. For example, I might not notice that I have left my office without the exam papers that I promised to return to my students because a fire alarm went off as I was packing my things up for class. Perhaps this excuses me in my students' eyes insofar as they regard my failure of attention as reasonable given relevant features of the situation in which I acted. I suspect, though, that the deeper explanation for the excuse is that, since my inadvertence is explained by a legitimate distraction, it is *not* explained by reference to something that would cast me in a worse moral light: namely, a lack of appropriate concern for attending to my promise and to my duties as a teacher. But note that it is perfectly conceivable that I might have forgotten the exam papers without the fire alarm going off (or anything similar happening) and yet my inadvertence might still not be explained by a lack of appropriate concern for my students – perhaps it just slipped my mind without this reflecting anything morally relevant about me. In this latter case, I think that I should still be excused, though I might have difficulty pointing my students to evidence in favor of excusing me.

Thus, with respect to Jeff, it seems to me that the question is what his failure to form accurate expectations about his self-forming choices tells us about him. If he had made self-forming choices *in full knowledge* of the general bad consequences of doing so, then it would be easy to see why he is to blame for bringing about these consequences. He would be blameworthy because his choice to develop traits that he knows will lead to bad consequences directly indicates his disregard for the moral quality of his choices and their consequences. However, if he really didn't recognize the moral status of his choices, then it will be far less clear that he disregards the moral status of his choices and their likely consequences. It's at least possible that, as a teenager, Jeff was about as concerned with making good choices as could be expected of him, but that he just didn't notice that the choices he was making were bad ones.

I suggest that, if Jeff was unaware of the potential consequences of his self-forming choices, there is room for skepticism about whether these choices can ground his blameworthiness for his later behavior, and this is because there is room for skepticism about whether his lack of awareness is explained by something that makes him blameworthy (such as a lack of concern for moral norms and for the needs and interests of other people). Perhaps what we need in order to be really confident that Jeff is blameworthy is not just to trace his non-deliberative choices as an adult back to bad deliberate choices – we may need to trace his non-deliberative choices back to *deliberately (that is, knowingly) bad* earlier choices.

5.4 Tracing and Attribution

As I said in the last section, I share some of Vargas's concerns about tracing. However, and despite my reflections in the preceding paragraphs, it seems to me that there are good grounds for regarding Jeff the Jerk as blameworthy and that we don't need to appeal to tracing to explain why this is so. (Though, as I argued above, if tracing were necessary for establishing blameworthiness in Jeff's case, we'd find a surer foundation for blame if we traced back to knowing wrongdoing.) Jeff is blameworthy – that is, he is open to blaming responses – because he is rude and insensitive. Regardless of whether he notices that he is insensitive, and regardless of whether he played a culpable role in turning himself into a callous jerk, Jeff's behavior likely expresses the sorts of objectionable judgments and attitudes to which blame is an appropriate response. There might be elements of his case that undermine the attribution of such judgments and attitudes to him, but none of the details that Vargas mentions has this tendency – certainly the fact that Jeff thinks he's "cool" doesn't have it. As Fischer and Tognazzini point out, "When you are a jerk to someone, your behavior is not excused by pointing out that you thought you were just doing the cool thing" (2009: 539).

The preceding, of course, exemplifies the approach an attributionist might take to Jeff's case: what makes him blameworthy is simply that his bad behavior is informed by objectionable judgments (even if merely implicit) about how others may be treated. On this view, there is no need to rely on tracing to explain Jeff's blameworthiness. As it happens, Fischer and Tognazzini are skeptical about this aspect of attributionism, particularly as it occurs in the work of Angela Smith.

Let's return to an example of Smith's that I mentioned in §2.5. In this example, Smith recalls a time when she forgot a close friend's birthday (2005: 236). Of course, she didn't *choose* to forget the birthday, but she still felt the need to apologize for her lapse, since it could be taken to indicate the presence of an objectionable evaluative judgment on her part: namely, that she judged her friend's feelings or happiness to be less important than she ought to have. On Smith's view, this judgment, if it existed, would provide adequate grounds for her friend's blame. Again, no tracing would be required – the objectionable evaluative judgment, which need not be the product of reflective (or even unreflective) choice, would be enough.[12]

Fischer and Tognazzini, by contrast, argue that, if Smith is blameworthy, "some sort of tracing must be going on in the birthday case," and their focus falls on the presumed "fact that Smith failed to choose to do various things which were such that, had she so chosen, she would have had a better chance of remembering her friend's birthday" (2009: 550). For example, she might have failed to record her friend's birthday on a calendar, and Fischer and Tognazzini claim that, "[i]f you don't take these steps...you are legitimately morally assessable for your forgetting *precisely because* you failed to do something to make your forgetting much less likely" (ibid.).

For Fischer and Tognazzini, it is only insofar as Smith's forgetting traces back to a benighting act (or omission) that she can be blamed for forgetting her friend's birthday. Despite this, they do not entirely reject her emphasis on the role that objectionable evaluative judgments play in blameworthiness. However, Fischer and Tognazzini appear to hold that the relevant objectionable judgments obtain only to the degree that the sort of trace they have in mind can be established: they say, for example, that "your forgetting reflects a poor evaluative judgment only insofar as you failed to take the necessary steps that any friend would take to remember friends' birthdays" (2009: 550).

But, on my view (and, I take it, on Smith's), while we might be able to trace Smith's forgetting back to a prior choice or omission of hers, this is not *why* she is blameworthy. Indeed, the reason we care about such a prior choice is because it might indicate something about Smith's evaluative commitments; otherwise, the prior choice would be irrelevant to blame. And, while a prior choice of Smith's might give us *evidence* that she holds an objectionable evaluative judgment, it is surely not necessary for the holding of such a judgment. Contrary to the tenor of Fischer and Tognazzini's discussion (2009: 550), it's at least possible that Smith's concern for her friend is morally deficient and that this explains why she forgot the birthday, and yet she did everything she could have been expected to do to remember the birthday.[13] It seems to me, in other words, that objectionable evaluative judgments might obtain without prior culpable actions – even if the latter are often a sign of the former – and, if such judgments are sufficient for blameworthiness, it is at least possible that some forgetful or inattentive agents are blameworthy without ever having committed a past culpable action.

Varieties of Attributionism

Some people object to attributionism on the grounds that it places too few conditions on blameworthiness and thus counts too many people as blameworthy – people helplessly born into slaveholding cultures, psychopaths, and so on (Levy 2005; Shoemaker 2011; Watson 2011). But, as I have articulated the view in this chapter, attributionism at least requires that a blameworthy agent possesses objectionable evaluative judgments or qualities of will. However, not all versions of attributionism share this feature. For example, on George Sher's approach, a person may be blameworthy for unwitting behavior regardless of whether it is linked to an objectionable judgment or whether it is expressive of ill will. It is enough for blame that a person's action has fallen below a relevant standard of care and that it is attributable to features of the agent that make her the sort of person she is – e.g., the agent's "constitutive attitudes, dispositions, and traits" (Sher 2009: 88; cf. Clarke 2014: 160–83).

In an example that Sher calls "Hot Dog," Alessandra leaves her dog Sheba in a car while she picks her children up at school. This is something that she does regularly and without incident. However, on this occasion Alessandra is unexpectedly delayed at the school by "a tangled tale of misbehavior, ill-considered punishment, and administrative bungling which requires several hours of indignant sorting out" (Sher 2009: 24). As a result, she forgets about Sheba in the hot car and the dog suffers heat prostration.

Is Alessandra blameworthy? On Sher's view, she probably is, but not necessarily because she "negligently failed to do something that would have prevented her from forgetting Sheba" (2009: 36). Alessandra is blameworthy simply because forgetting Sheba falls below the standard of care a person owes to her pet and because her forgetting is attributable to facts about the kind of person she is – for example, facts about the degree to which she is "solicitous of her children" or made "anxious by conflict" (ibid.: 92).

Sher's approach casts a very wide net indeed. Not only is Alessandra's blameworthiness independent of whether her lapse can be traced back to a benighting choice, it doesn't even matter whether her lapse is traceable to an independent moral defect. (Being solicitous of one's children or being made anxious by conflict are not prominent moral faults.) Sher takes Alessandra's supposed blameworthiness to be a counter-example to views like Angela Smith's that require blame to be grounded in an objectionable attitude or quality of will (Sher 2009: 131). However, it seems quite reasonable to me to say that Alessandra is not blameworthy if her forgetting Sheba is not explained by a moral fault such as a condemnable lack of concern for the dog's welfare. Of course, Alessandra's lapse means that her care for Sheba has been less than ideal: it certainly would have been better if she had not forgotten about her. This is what allows Sher to characterize Alessandra as a wrongdoer. But, in my view, this counts as wrongdoing only in a weak sense and, if the wrong done by Alessandra is not indicative of a trait or orientation that is independently morally objectionable, I don't see how it can ground true moral blameworthiness (Talbert 2011: 150–1).

On the other hand, if you agree with Sher that Alessandra is open to moral blame, then it will count as a limitation of other attributionist views (like Smith's) that they have trouble explaining how this can be so. Related concerns arise in other contexts. Think back to cases of drunk driving: Are drunk drivers blameworthy on the kind of view Angela Smith advocates? This would be so only if we can find some objectionable quality of will, attitude, or judgment upon which to hang the driver's blame. We might say, for example, that, in choosing to drink in a context in which he might later drive, the driver is guilty of a condemnable lack of concern for how his behavior will affect other people. But what if we think the drunk driver is *very* blameworthy because his driving led to very bad consequences? In this case, we might worry that the blame-grounding lack of concern to which we can trace the driver's behavior is not proportionate to the degree of blame that we feel he deserves. At this point we could conclude either that the drunk driver is less blameworthy than we might have thought or that at least this form of attributionism does not give us the right result in some cases (the problem here is related to the difficulty of accounting for moral luck in outcomes, which I discussed in §3.1).

The more general problem for attributionism, to which the drunk driving example points, is in dealing with cases of negligence. We commonly think that thoughtless or heedless people are blameworthy for the damage that their inattention causes. But it may be hard to pin an appropriately bad quality of will on an agent who is simply not paying attention. Of course, it's trivially true that, when she is not aware of the likely bad consequences of her actions or omissions, a person's degree of concern was not sufficient to ensure that she noticed whatever it was that she didn't notice. But, as I argued above, it does not necessarily follow that the agent in such a case displayed the kind of disregard for others that is necessary for blameworthiness. Sometimes (and perhaps very often) our failures to notice or to remember things don't indicate much about how we are oriented toward others: indeed, we sometimes forget or fail to notice things about which we care very much.

This suggests to me that, if we accept attributionism, we will have reason to be skeptical about blameworthiness in some garden-variety cases of failures of awareness. The problem is that our everyday moral practices don't seem to evince much skepticism in this domain. So, again, we must either conclude that the form of attributionism I advocate gives us the wrong result in some cases or that a common feature of everyday moral practice is to some degree mistaken.

5.5   Conclusion

The material in this chapter is related in several ways to the concerns about personal history and moral competence raised in the last two chapters. For example, a central way in which an agent's moral competence may be impaired is that her access to moral knowledge is limited by her present values and beliefs. Mr Potter's bad values and moral ignorance seem to impair his competence in this way: given his commitment to a flawed moral outlook, it may not be reasonable to expect him to conduct himself better than he does. Of course, Mr Potter has a flawed moral outlook largely because of some combination of facts about his upbringing and facts about his initial constitution, neither of which he chose. In addition, the skeptical argument presented in this chapter is structurally similar to the one defended by Galen Strawson ([1994] 2003) in §3.2. Both positions rely on the idea that we are blameworthy for our present wrongdoing (or, in the case of this chapter, our present unwitting wrongdoing) only insofar as it is the result of some crucial initial contribution that we have made: an original self-forming choice in Strawson's case or an initial instance of knowing wrongdoing in the cases of Gideon Rosen and Michael Zimmerman. Arguments about tracing of course also revolve around the supposed need, in some cases, for referring to past acts in order to ground responsibility for present behavior.

With respect to these issues and others, I have made largely the same attributionist point. When it comes to assessing a wrongdoer's blameworthiness, it doesn't matter whether she could have been expected to conduct herself differently or whether facts about her history and moral competence determined that she would regard her bad behavior as choiceworthy. What matters is whether a person has governed her behavior in a way that reflects an objectionable orientation toward others and a misevaluation of how the needs and interests of others ought to be weighed in practical reasoning. When a person governs her bad behavior like this, it is attributable to her in a way that licenses not just a negative moral assessment but also the responses that normally characterize moral blame. This form of self-government seems compatible with agents finding themselves in many of the predicaments described in this and earlier chapters.

I regard the approach I take as a hard-line (though I hope not hard-hearted) compatibilism and as the natural outcome of taking seriously Harry Frankfurt's proposal (§1.5) that "what really counts [for moral responsibility] is not whether an action was avoidable but in what way it came to be that the action was performed" (2006: 340), together with P. F. Strawson's observation (§2.2) that what attracts our attention in assessing responsibility is whether a person's behavior reflects toward us attitudes of good or ill will ([1963] 1993). Taking these compatibilist perspectives seriously leads us, I believe, to accept many of the conclusions for which I have argued. Of course, to the degree that these conclusions seem incredible – that is, to the degree that psychopaths, people with deficient moral educations, and victims of manipulation seem not to be responsible (at least not on the grounds that I propose) – this may serve as a *reductio* of my view (and perhaps of certain forms of compatibilism more generally).

5.6 Further Reading

Important book-length treatments of the epistemic dimension of moral responsibility include Sher (2009) and Zimmerman (2008). Readers should also see Clarke (2014: 160–83) and Levy (2011b: 110–32). For additional responses to the Rosen–Zimmerman thesis regarding akrasia and responsibility, see Guerrero (2007), Harman (2011), and Mason (2015). At the end of §5.4, I described certain problems that can arise for attributionism in the context of negligence; related concerns are addressed by King (2009), Levy (2011a), and Smith (2011). Other important philosophical treatments of negligence include Sverdlik (1993) and Zimmerman (1986), and, in 2011, the journal *Criminal Law and Philosophy* devoted an entire issue to the subject (vol. 5:2). For more on tracing, see Khoury (2012), King (2011), Shabo (2014), and Timpe (2011).

Notes

1 The sort of view I have in mind is exemplified, to varying degrees, by Adams (1985), Arpaly (2003), Hieronymi (2004, 2008a), Scanlon (1998, 2008), Sher (2006, 2009), Smith (2005, 2008), and Talbert (2012a, 2013, 2014).

2 As remarked by a reviewer for Polity, it's possible to interpret Sher as giving a watered-down account of blame, perhaps too watered-down for it to plausibly capture the accountability side of blame. After all, and as I've noted, for Sher, one can blame without being subject to emotions such as resentment. However, while Sher believes "that blame is not always accompanied by hard feelings," he acknowledges that it often is: "When we blame someone, we may feel – among other things – anger, resentment, irritation, bitterness, hostility" (Sher 2006: 94). I take it that, when Sher argues that blame can be legitimized on (what I identify as) attributionist grounds, he means that the foregoing responses, which are associated with accountability blame, are at least sometimes appropriate. (On the other hand, it's also possible to develop a version of Sher's view that dispenses with these responses: see Hieronymi 2008b: 25; Pereboom 2014: 130–1.) I take a similar point to apply to the views of the other two authors I discuss in this section (Angela Smith and T. M. Scanlon). While neither talks about resentment (etc.) at great length (and Scanlon often emphasizes other forms that blame can take), they both clearly regard resentment to be a blaming response that is sometimes permitted on attributionist grounds.

3 As Nagel notes ([1976] 1979: 38 n.12), there is some similarity between the point he's making here and Strawson's discussion

of the "objective perspective" which we encountered in the previous chapter.

4   Kane's UR condition focuses on choices and actions that have sufficient causes: that is, cases in which the presence of certain causal antecedents guarantees the occurrence of a particular choice. However, a skeptic about moral responsibility might say that ultimate responsibility requires responsibility for the reasons, motives, and desires that causally influence our choices regardless of whether they determine those choices. For an account of how the presence of non-deterministic causes creates problems for Kane's variety of libertarianism, see Pereboom (2001: 47–50).

5   Historical conditions on responsibility might require agents to have made a certain contribution to their own development, or they might simply require that responsibility-undermining influences were absent. For this distinction, see David Zimmerman (2003: 646–8).

6   A requirement along these (or importantly related) lines plays a role in Benson (1987), Fischer and Ravizza (1998), Levy (2011b), McKenna (2012), Nelkin (2011), Russell (2004), Wallace (1996), Watson (2004a), and Wolf (1987, 1990), among many other examples.

7   I say that the fairness of resentment has *mainly* to do with the attributability of wrongdoing because we should keep in mind the difference explored in §2.6 between judging that a person is blameworthy and actively blaming her.

8   As Nelkin notes, Doris and Murphy (2007) develop this line of thought with explicit application to war crimes; for a reply, see Talbert (2009b).

9   This obscures some of the complexity of Shoemaker's view: he believes that psychopaths can be blamed for their behavior in a limited way, but not in the way that would make attitudes such as moral resentment appropriate.

10 The contrast between control and epistemic conditions is illuminating, but it is probably best not to insist on a strict division between the two since they seem to intersect in various ways. It is natural, for example, to think of ignorance as something that can limit control: we lack at least some form of control over our behavior when we don't know what we are doing. Aristotle's way of formulating the distinction suggests as much: since what is involuntary is (in some important sense) not in our control, then, if ignorance undermines voluntariness, it also undermines control. For related reflections, see Mele (2010).

11 There is a sense of "expectation" in which it is unreasonable to expect someone to do something when she cannot do it (or when she cannot recognize the force of the considerations that count in favor of doing it). Attributionists do not regard blame as necessarily expressing expectations in this sense of the word. However, we could also speak of expectations as merely expressing our views about how it is morally preferable for a person to behave. Expectations, in this sense of the word, make no assumptions about a person's ability to live up to them. Attributionists would be free to interpret blame as expressing an expectation in this second sense.

12 Smith accepts the point I emphasized in the last section: that not all cases of forgetting, or of failing to notice, are related to judgments that ground blame (2005: 244 n.14). However, it may be that we disagree about how far to apply this insight. For example, as I read the birthday case, Smith may not be blameworthy at all: perhaps she cares for her friend very much and simply forgot the birthday, without this telling us anything deeper about Smith's values and attitudes. Now, even if this were true, it would still be natural for Smith to apologize in order to assure her friend that she cares for her as much as she ought to – though, in the absence of blameworthiness, "apologize" might not be quite the right word.

13 Of course, the most obvious explanation for why Smith would take steps to remember the birthday is that she cares for her friend; it can therefore be difficult to think of a case in which she takes these steps, yet her degree of concern is deficient. Still, the right sort of case is certainly conceivable: perhaps Smith habitually takes steps to remember the birthdays of all her acquaintances regardless of how she feels about them. Or suppose that she has an excellent memory for the birthdays of people for whom she cares deeply. In this case, she might reasonably fail to take any special steps to remember the birthday, since she reasonably believes that she cares deeply for the person in question. However, Smith might forget the birthday because it turns out that she doesn't care for this person as much as she ought to and as much as she thought she did.

References

Adams, Robert (1985) "Involuntary Sins," *Philosophical Review* 94: 3–31.

Aristotle (1999) *Nicomachean Ethics*, ed. and trans. T. Irwin. Indianapolis: Hackett.

Arpaly, Nomy (2003) *Unprincipled Virtue: An Inquiry into Moral Agency*. New York: Oxford University Press.

Babiak, Paul, and Robert Hare (2006) *Snakes in Suits: When Psychopaths Go to Work*. New York: HarperCollins.

Babiak, Paul, et al. (2010) "Corporate Psychopathy: Talking the Walk," *Behavioral Sciences and the Law* 28: 174–93.

Bell, Macalester (2013) "The Standing to Blame: A Critique," in D. Coates and N. Tognazzini (eds), *Blame: Its Nature and Norms*. New York: Oxford University Press, pp. 263–81.

Bennett, Christopher (2013) "The Expressive Function of Blame," in D. Coates and N. Tognazzini (eds), *Blame: Its Nature and Norms*. New York: Oxford University Press, pp. 66–83.

Benson, Paul (1987) "Freedom and Value," *Journal of Philosophy* 84: 465–86.

Benson, Paul (2001) "Culture and Responsibility: A Reply to Moody-Adams," *Journal of Social Philosophy* 32: 610–20.

Berofsky, Bernard (ed.) (1966) *Free Will and Determinism*. New York: Harper & Row.

Blair, James, et al. (2005) *The Psychopath: Emotion and the Brain*. Oxford: Blackwell.

Campbell, C. A. ([1951] 1966) "Is Freewill a Pseudo-Problem," in B. Berofsky (ed.), *Free Will and Determinism*. New York: Harper & Row, pp. 112–35.

Campbell, Joseph Keim (2011) *Free Will.* Cambridge: Polity.

Chisholm, Roderick ([1964] 2003) "Human Freedom and the Self," in G. Watson (ed.), *Free Will.* 2nd edn, New York: Oxford University Press, pp. 26–37.

Clarke, Randolph (2003) *Libertarian Accounts of Free Will.* New York: Oxford University Press.

Clarke, Randolph (2014) *Omissions: Agency, Metaphysics, and Responsibility.* New York: Oxford University Press.

Clarke, Randolph, and Justin Capes (2014) "Incompatibilist (Non-deterministic) Theories of Free Will," in E. N. Zalta (ed.), *The Stanford Encyclopedia of Philosophy*, http://plato.stanford.edu/archives/spr2014/entries/incompatibilism-theories/.

Cleckley, Hervey ([1941] 1976) *The Mask of Sanity.* 5th edn, St Louis, MO: Mosby.

Coates, D. Justin, and Neal A. Tognazzini (2013a) "The Contours of Blame," in D. Coates and N. Tognazzini (eds), *Blame: Its Nature and Norms.* New York: Oxford University Press, pp. 3–26.

Coates, D. Justin, and Neal A. Tognazzini (eds) (2013b) *Blame: Its Nature and Norms.* New York: Oxford University Press.

D'Arms, Justin, and Daniel Jacobson (2003) "The Significance of Recalcitrant Emotion (or, Anti-quasijudgmentalism)," in A. Hatzimoysis (ed.), *Philosophy and the Emotions.* Cambridge: Cambridge University Press, pp. 127–45.

Darwall, Stephen (2006) *The Second-Person Standpoint: Morality, Respect, and Accountability.* Cambridge, MA: Harvard University Press.

Demetriou, Kristin (2010) "The Soft-Line Solution to Pereboom's Four-Case Argument," *Australasian Journal of Philosophy* 88: 595–617.

Doris, John (2002) *Lack of Character: Personality and Moral Behavior.* Cambridge: Cambridge University Press.

Doris, John, and Dominic Murphy (2007) "From My Lai to Abu Ghraib: The Moral Psychology of Atrocity," *Midwest Studies in Philosophy* 31: 25–55.

Dworkin, Gerald (ed.) (1970a) *Determinism, Free Will, and Moral Responsibility.* Englewood Cliffs, NJ: Prentice-Hall.

Dworkin, Gerald (1970b) "Acting Freely," *Noûs* 4: 367–83.

Ekstrom, Laura (2000) *Free Will: A Philosophical Study.* Boulder, CO: Westview Press.

Eshleman, Andrew (2014) "Moral Responsibility," in E. N. Zalta (ed.), *The Stanford Encyclopedia of Philosophy*, http://plato.stanford.edu/archives/sum2014/entries/moral-responsibility/.

Fine, Cordelia, and Jeanette Kennett (2004) "Mental Impairment, Moral Understanding and Criminal Responsibility: Psychopathy and the Purposes of Punishment," *International Journal of Law and Psychiatry* 27: 425–43.

Fischer, John Martin ([2003] 2006a) "Responsibility and Alternative Possibilities," in J. Fischer, *My Way: Essays on Moral Responsibility*. New York: Oxford University Press, pp. 38–62.

Fischer, John Martin ([2002] 2006b) "Frankfurt-Style Compatibilism," in J. Fischer, *My Way: Essays on Moral Responsibility*. New York: Oxford University Press, pp. 124–42.

Fischer, John Martin (2006c) "The Cards That are Dealt You," *Journal of Ethics* 10: 107–29.

Fischer, John Martin (2010) "The Frankfurt Cases: The Moral of the Stories," *Philosophical Review* 119: 315–36.

Fischer, John Martin, and Mark Ravizza (1993) "Introduction," in J. Fischer and M. Ravizza (eds), *Perspectives on Moral Responsibility*. Ithaca, NY: Cornell University Press, pp. 1–41.

Fischer, John Martin, and Mark Ravizza (1998) *Responsibility and Control: A Theory of Moral Responsibility*. Cambridge: Cambridge University Press.

Fischer, John Martin, and Neal Tognazzini (2009) "The Truth about Tracing," *Noûs* 43: 531–56.

FitzPatrick, William J. (2008) "Moral Responsibility and Normative Ignorance: Answering a New Skeptical Challenge," *Ethics* 118: 589–613.

Foot, Philippa (1957) "Free Will as Involving Determinism," *Philosophical Review* 66: 439–50.

Frankfurt, Harry ([1969] 1988a) "Alternate Possibilities and Moral Responsibility," in H. Frankfurt, *The Importance of What We Care About*. Cambridge: Cambridge University Press, pp. 1–10.

Frankfurt, Harry ([1971] 1988b) "Freedom of the Will and the Concept of a Person," in H. Frankfurt, *The Importance of What We Care About*. Cambridge: Cambridge University Press, pp. 11–25.

Frankfurt, Harry ([1987] 1988c) "Identification and Wholeheartedness," in H. Frankfurt, *The Importance of What We Care About*. Cambridge: Cambridge University Press, pp. 159–76.

Frankfurt, Harry (2006) "Some Thoughts Concerning PAP," in D. Widerker and M. McKenna (eds.), *Moral Responsibility and Alternative Possibilities: Essays on the Importance of Alternative Possibilities*. Burlington, VT: Ashgate, pp. 339–445.

Franklin, Christopher (2013) "Valuing Blame," in D. Coates and N. Tognazzini (eds), *Blame: Its Nature and Norms*. New York: Oxford University Press, pp. 207–23.

Glannon, Walter (1997) "Psychopathy and Responsibility," *Journal of Applied Ethics* 14: 263–75.

Glover, Jonathan (1970) *Responsibility*. London: Routledge & Kegan Paul.

Goodwyn, Wade (interviewer) (2013) "What One GOP Congressman Would Do about Syria," *Weekend Edition Sunday*, September 1, www.npr.org/2013/09/01/217841118/what-one-gop-congressman-would-do-about-syria.

Greenspan, Patricia (2003) "Responsible Psychopaths," *Philosophical Psychology* 16: 417–29.

Guerrero, Alexander A. (2007) "Don't Know, Don't Kill: Moral Ignorance, Culpability, and Caution," *Philosophical Studies* 136: 59–97.

Haji, Ishtiyaque (1998) *Moral Appraisability*. New York: Oxford University Press.

Hare, Robert D. (1993) *Without Conscience: The Disturbing World of the Psychopaths among Us*. New York: Guilford Press.

Harman, Elizabeth (2011) "Does Moral Ignorance Exculpate?," *Ratio* 24: 443–68.

Hart, H. L. A. (1968) "Postscript: Responsibility and Retribution," in H. Hart, *Punishment and Responsibility: Essays in the Philosophy of Law*. Oxford: Oxford University Press, pp. 210–37.

Hieronymi, Pamela (2001) "Articulating an Uncompromising Forgiveness," *Philosophy and Phenomenological Research* 62: 529–55.

Hieronymi, Pamela (2004) "The Force and Fairness of Blame," *Philosophical Topics* 18: 115–48.

Hieronymi, Pamela (2008a) "Responsibility for Believing," *Synthese* 161: 357–73.

Hieronymi, Pamela (2008b) "Sher's Defense of Blame," *Philosophical Studies* 137: 19–30.

Hobart, R. E. (1934) "Free Will as Involving Determination and Inconceivable Without It," *Mind* 43: 1–27.

Hook, Sidney (ed.) (1961) *Determinism and Freedom in the Age of Modern Science*. New York: Collier Books.

Hunt, David (2000) "Moral Responsibility and Unavoidable Action," *Philosophical Studies* 97: 195–227.

Kane, Robert (1996) *The Significance of Free Will*. New York: Oxford University Press.

Kane, Robert (2005) *A Contemporary Introduction to Free Will*. New York: Oxford University Press.

Kane, Robert (2007) "Libertarianism," in J. Fischer et al., *Four Views on Free Will*. Oxford: Blackwell, pp. 5–43.

Kant, Immanuel ([1788] 1997) *Critique of Practical Reason*, ed. and trans. M. Gregor. Cambridge: Cambridge University Press.

Kelly, Erin (2013) "What Is an Excuse?" in D. Coates and N. Tognazzini (eds), *Blame: Its Nature and Norms.* New York: Oxford University Press, pp. 244–62.

Khoury, Andrew (2012) "Responsibility, Tracing, and Consequences," *Canadian Journal of Philosophy* 42: 187–207.

Khoury, Andrew (2013) "Synchronic and Diachronic Responsibility," *Philosophical Studies* 165: 735–52.

King, Matt (2009) "The Problem with Negligence," *Social Theory and Practice* 35: 577–95.

King, Matt (2011) "Traction without Tracing: A (Partial) Solution for Control-Based Accounts of Moral Responsibility," *European Journal of Philosophy* 22: 463–82.

Lehrer, Keith (1968) "Cans Without Ifs," *Analysis* 29: 29–32.

Levy, Neil (2003) "Cultural Membership and Moral Responsibility," *The Monist* 86: 145–63.

Levy, Neil (2005) "The Good, the Bad and the Blameworthy," *Journal of Ethics and Social Philosophy* 1: 1–16.

Levy, Neil (2007) "The Responsibility of the Psychopath Revisited," *Philosophy, Psychiatry, and Psychology* 14: 129–38.

Levy, Neil (2009) "Culpable Ignorance and Moral Responsibility: A Reply to FitzPatrick," *Ethics* 119: 729–41.

Levy, Neil (2011a) "Expressing Who We Are: Moral Responsibility and Awareness of Our Reasons for Action," *Analytic Philosophy* 52: 243–61.

Levy, Neil (2011b) *Hard Luck: How Luck Undermines Free Will and Moral Responsibility.* New York: Oxford University Press.

Lewis, David ([1981] 2003) "Are We Free to Break the Laws," in G. Watson (ed.), *Free Will.* 2nd edn, New York: Oxford University Press, pp. 122–9.

Litton, Paul (2010) "Psychopathy and Responsibility Theory," *Philosophy Compass* 5: 676–88.

Lucas, J. R. (1993) *Responsibility.* New York: Oxford University Press.

Macnamara, Coleen (2013) "Taking Demands Out of Blame," in D. Coates and N. Tognazzini (eds), *Blame: Its Nature and Norms.* New York: Oxford University Press, pp. 141–61.

Maibom, Heidi (2008) "The Mad, the Bad, and the Psychopath," *Neuroethics* 1: 167–84.

Malatesti, Luca, and John McMillan (eds) (2010) *Responsibility and Psychopathy: Interfacing Law, Psychiatry and Philosophy.* New York: Oxford University Press.

Marx, Karl ([1852] 1972) *The Eighteenth Brumaire of Louis Napoleon,* in R. Tucker (ed.), *The Marx–Engels Reader.* New York: W. W. Norton.

Mason, Elinor (2015) "Moral Ignorance and Blameworthiness," *Philosophical Studies*, doi: 10.1007/s11098-015-0456-7.

Matheson, Benjamin (2014) "Compatibilism and Personal Identity," *Philosophical Studies* 170: 317–34.

McGeer, Victoria (2013) "Civilizing Blame," in D. Coates and N. Tognazzini (eds), *Blame: Its Nature and Norms*. New York: Oxford University Press, pp. 162–88.

McKenna, Michael (2004) "Responsibility and Globally Manipulated Agents," *Philosophical Topics* 32: 169–92.

McKenna, Michael (2008) "A Hard-Line Reply to Pereboom's Four-Case Argument," *Philosophy and Phenomenological Research* 77: 142–59.

McKenna, Michael (2012) *Conversation and Responsibility*. New York: Oxford University Press.

McKenna, Michael, and D. Justin Coates (2015) "Compatibilism," in E. N. Zalta (ed.), *The Stanford Encyclopedia of Philosophy*, http://plato.stanford.edu/archives/spr2015/entries/compatibilism/.

McKenna, Michael, and Paul Russell (eds) (2008) *Free Will and Reactive Attitudes: Perspectives on P. F. Strawson's "Freedom and Resentment."* Farnham: Ashgate.

Mele, Alfred (1995) *Autonomous Agents: From Self-Control to Autonomy*. New York: Oxford University Press.

Mele, Alfred (2006) *Free Will and Luck*. New York: Oxford University Press.

Mele, Alfred (2010) "Moral Responsibility for Actions: Epistemic and Freedom Conditions," *Philosophical Explorations* 13: 101–11.

Mele, Alfred (2014) *Free: Why Science Hasn't Disproved Free Will*. New York: Oxford University Press.

Mele, Alfred, and David Robb (1998) "Rescuing Frankfurt-Style Cases," *Philosophical Review* 107: 97–112.

Milgram, Stanley (1969) *Obedience to Authority*. New York: Harper & Row.

Moody-Adams, Michele (1990) "On the Old Saw that Character is Destiny," in O. Flanagan and A. Rorty (eds), *Identity, Character, and Morality: Essays in Moral Psychology*. Cambridge, MA: MIT Press, pp. 111–32.

Moore, G. E. (1912) *Ethics*. Oxford: Oxford University Press.

Muskal, Michael (2013) "Texas Teen's Probation for Killing 4 While Driving Drunk Stirs Anger," *Los Angeles Times*, December 12, http://articles.latimes.com/2013/dec/12/nation/la-na-nn-texas-teen-drunk-driving-probation-affluenza-20131212.

Nagel, Thomas ([1976] 1979) "Moral Luck," in T. Nagel, *Mortal Questions*. Cambridge: Cambridge University Press, pp. 24–38.

Neely, Wright (1974) "Freedom and Desire," *Philosophical Review* 83: 32–54.

Nelkin, Dana (2005) "Freedom, Responsibility and the Challenge of Situationism," *Midwest Studies in Philosophy* 29: 181–206.

Nelkin, Dana (2011) *Making Sense of Freedom and Responsibility*. New York: Oxford University Press.

Nelkin, Dana (2013) "Moral Luck," in E. N. Zalta (ed.), *The Stanford Encyclopedia of Philosophy*, http://plato.stanford.edu/archives/win2013/entries/moral-luck/.

Nelkin, Dana (2015) "Psychopaths, Incorrigible Racists, and the Faces of Responsibility," *Ethics* 125: 357–90.

Nichols, Shaun (2002) "How Psychopaths Threaten Moral Rationalism: Is it Irrational to be Amoral?" *The Monist* 85: 285–304.

O'Connor, Timothy (2000) *Persons and Causes*. New York: Oxford University Press.

O'Connor, Timothy (2014) "Free Will," in E. N. Zalta (ed.), *The Stanford Encyclopedia of Philosophy*, http://plato.stanford.edu/archives/fall2014/entries/freewill/.

Oshana, Marina (2004) "Moral Accountability," *Philosophical Topics* 32: 255–74.

Pereboom, Derk (1995) "Determinism *Al Dente*," *Noûs* 29: 21–45.

Pereboom, Derk (2001) *Living Without Free Will*. Cambridge: Cambridge University Press.

Pereboom, Derk (2007) "Hard Incompatibilism," in J. Fischer et al., *Four Views on Free Will*. Oxford: Blackwell, pp. 85–125.

Pereboom, Derk (2014) *Free Will, Agency, and Meaning in Life*. New York: Oxford University Press.

Pettit, Philip (2001) *A Theory of Freedom: From the Psychology to the Politics of Agency*. New York: Oxford University Press.

Rosen, Gideon (2003) "Culpability and Ignorance," *Proceedings of the Aristotelian Society* 103: 61–84.

Rosen, Gideon (2004) "Skepticism about Moral Responsibility," *Philosophical Perspectives* 18: 295–313.

Rosen, Gideon (2008) "Kleinbart the Oblivious and Other Tales of Ignorance and Responsibility," *Journal of Philosophy* 105: 591–610.

Russell, Paul (1992) "Strawson's Way of Naturalizing Responsibility," *Ethics* 102: 287–302.

Russell, Paul (2004) "Responsibility and the Condition of Moral Sense," *Philosophical Topics* 32: 287–306.

Russell, Paul, and Oisín Deery (eds) (2013) *The Philosophy of Free Will: Essential Readings from the Contemporary Debates*. New York: Oxford University Press.

Ryan, Chris (2013) "Chip Kelly and the Eagles Are Here to Make Football Fun Again," September 10, www.grantland.com/blog/the-triangle/post/_/id/73986/chip-kelly-and-the-eagles-are-here-to-make-football-fun-again.

Scanlon, T. M. (1998) *What We Owe to Each Other*. Cambridge, MA: Harvard University Press.

Scanlon, T. M. (2008) *Moral Dimensions: Permissibility, Meaning, and Blame*. Cambridge, MA: Harvard University Press.

Schlick, Moritz ([1930] 1966) "When is a Man Responsible?" in B. Berofsky (ed.), *Free Will and Determinism*. New York: Harper & Row, pp. 54–63.

Schramme, Thomas (ed.) (2014) *Being Amoral: Psychopathy and Moral Incapacity*. Cambridge MA: MIT Press.

Shabo, Seth (2010) "Uncompromising Source Incompatibilism," *Philosophy and Phenomenological Research* 80: 349–83.

Shabo, Seth (2014) "More Trouble with Tracing," *Erkenntnis*, doi: 10.1007/s10670-014-9693-y.

Sher, George (2006) *In Praise of Blame*. New York: Oxford University Press.

Sher, George (2009) *Who Knew?: Responsibility Without Awareness*. New York: Oxford University Press.

Shoemaker, David (2011) "Attributability, Answerability, and Accountability: Toward a Wider Theory of Moral Responsibility," *Ethics* 121: 602–32.

Shoemaker, David (2012) "Responsibility Without Identity," *Harvard Review of Philosophy* 18: 108–132.

Shoemaker, David (ed.) (2013) *Oxford Studies in Agency and Responsibility*, Vol. 1. Oxford: Oxford University Press.

Shoemaker, David (2014) "Psychopathy, Responsibility, and the Moral/Conventional Distinction," in T. Schramme (ed.), *Being Amoral: Psychopathy and Moral Incapacity*. Cambridge, MA: MIT Press, pp. 247–74.

Shoemaker, David, and Tognazzini, Neal (eds) (2014) *Oxford Studies in Agency and Responsibility*, Vol. 2: *"Freedom and Resentment" at 50*. Oxford: Oxford University Press.

Skinner, B. F. ([1948] 1962) *Walden Two*. New York: Macmillan.

Smart, J. J. C. (1973) "An Outline of a Utilitarian System of Ethics," in J. Smart and B. Williams, *Utilitarianism: For and Against*. Cambridge: Cambridge University Press, pp. 3–74.

Smart, J. J. C. ([1961] 2003) "Free Will, Praise, and Blame," in G. Watson (ed.), *Free Will*. 2nd edn, New York: Oxford University Press, pp. 58–71.

Smilansky, Saul (2000) *Free Will and Illusion*. New York: Oxford University Press.

Smith, Angela (2005) "Responsibility for Attitudes: Activity and Passivity in Mental Life," *Ethics* 115: 236–71.

Smith, Angela (2007) "On Being Responsible and Holding Responsible," *Journal of Ethics* 11: 465–84.

Smith, Angela (2008) "Control, Responsibility, and Moral Assessment," *Philosophical Studies* 138: 367–92.

Smith, Angela (2012) "Attributability, Answerability, and Accountability: In Defense of a Unified Account," *Ethics* 122: 575–89.

Smith, Angela (2013) "Moral Blame and Moral Protest," in D. Coates and N. Tognazzini (eds), *Blame: Its Nature and Norms*. New York: Oxford University Press, pp. 27–48.

Smith, Holly (1983) "Culpable Ignorance," *Philosophical Review* 92: 543–71.

Smith, Holly (2011) "Non-Tracing Cases of Culpable Ignorance," *Criminal Law and Philosophy* 5: 115–46.

Statman, Daniel (ed.) (1993) *Moral Luck*. Albany: State University of New York Press.

Strawson, Galen ([1986] 1993) "On Freedom and Resentment," in J. Fischer and M. Ravizza (eds), *Perspectives on Moral Responsibility*. Ithaca, NY: Cornell University Press, pp. 67–100.

Strawson, Galen ([1994] 2003) "The Impossibility of Moral Responsibility," in G. Watson (ed.), *Free Will*. 2nd edn, New York: Oxford University Press, pp. 212–28.

Strawson, P. F. ([1963] 1993) "Freedom and Resentment," in J. Fischer and M. Ravizza (eds), *Perspectives on Moral Responsibility*. Ithaca, NY: Cornell University Press, pp. 45–66.

Sverdlik, Steven (1993) "Pure Negligence," *American Philosophical Quarterly* 30: 137–49.

Talbert, Matthew (2008) "Blame and Responsiveness to Moral Reasons: Are Psychopaths Blameworthy?" *Pacific Philosophical Quarterly* 89: 516–35.

Talbert, Matthew (2009a) "Implanted Desires, Self-Formation and Blame," *Journal of Ethics & Social Philosophy* 3: 1–18.

Talbert, Matthew (2009b) "Situationism, Normative Competence, and Responsibility for Wartime Behavior," *Journal of Value Inquiry* 43: 415–32.

Talbert, Matthew (2011) "Unwitting Behavior and Responsibility," *Journal of Moral Philosophy* 8: 139–52.

Talbert, Matthew (2012a) "Moral Competence, Moral Blame, and Protest," *Journal of Ethics* 16: 89–109.

Talbert, Matthew (2012b) "Accountability, Aliens, and Psychopaths: A Reply to Shoemaker," *Ethics* 122: 562–74.

Talbert, Matthew (2013) "Unwitting Wrongdoers and the Role of Moral Disagreement in Blame," in D. Shoemaker (ed.), *Oxford*

Studies in Agency and Responsibility, Vol. 1. Oxford: Oxford University Press, pp. 225–45.

Talbert, Matthew (2014) "The Significance of Psychopathic Wrong-doing," in T. Schramme (ed.), *Being Amoral: Psychopathy and Moral Incapacity*. Cambridge, MA: MIT Press, pp. 275–300.

Timpe, Kevin (2011) "Tracing and the Epistemic Condition on Moral Responsibility," *Modern Schoolman* 88: 5–28.

Tognazzini, Neal A., and D. Justin Coates (2014) "Blame," in E. N. Zalta (ed.), *The Stanford Encyclopedia of Philosophy*, http://plato.stanford.edu/archives/sum2014/entries/blame/.

van Inwagen, Peter (1983) *An Essay on Free Will*. New York: Oxford University Press.

van Inwagen, Peter (2009) *Metaphysics*. Boulder, CO: Westview Press.

Vargas, Manuel (2005) "The Trouble with Tracing," *Midwest Studies in Philosophy* 29: 269–91.

Vargas, Manuel (2006) "On the Importance of History for Responsible Agency," *Philosophical Studies* 127: 351–82.

Vargas, Manuel (2013) "Situationism and Moral Responsibility: Free Will in Fragments," in A. Clark et al. (eds), *Decomposing the Will*. New York: Oxford University Press, pp. 325–50.

Vargas, Manuel, and Shaun Nichols (2007) "Psychopaths and Moral Knowledge," *Philosophy, Psychiatry, and Psychology* 14: 157–62.

Velleman, David J. (1992) "What Happens When Someone Acts?" *Mind* 101: 461–81.

Vihvelin, Kadri (2011) "Arguments for Incompatibilism," in E. N. Zalta (ed.), *The Stanford Encyclopedia of Philosophy*, http://plato.stanford.edu/archives/spr2011/entries/incompatibilism-arguments/.

Wallace, R. Jay (1996) *Responsibility and the Moral Sentiments*. Cambridge, MA: Harvard University Press.

Wallace, R. Jay (2013) "Rightness and Responsibility," in D. Coates and N. Tognazzini (eds), *Blame: Its Nature and Norms*. New York: Oxford University Press, pp. 224–43.

Wallace, R. Jay, Rahul Kumar, and Samuel Freeman (eds) (2011) *Reasons and Recognition: Essays on the Philosophy of T. M. Scanlon*. New York: Oxford University Press.

Waller, Bruce (2011) *Against Moral Responsibility*. Cambridge, MA: MIT Press.

Watson, Gary (1975) "Free Agency," *Journal of Philosophy* 72: 205–20.

Watson, Gary (2002) "Contractualism and the Boundaries of Morality: Remarks on Scanlon's *What We Owe to Each Other*," *Social Theory and Practice* 28: 221–41.

Watson, Gary (ed.) (2003) *Free Will.* 2nd edn, New York: Oxford University Press.

Watson, Gary ([1987] 2004a) "Responsibility and the Limits of Evil: Variations on a Strawsonian Theme," in G. Watson, *Agency and Answerability: Selected Essays.* New York: Oxford University Press, pp. 219–59.

Watson, Gary ([1996] 2004b) "Two Faces of Responsibility," in G. Watson, *Agency and Answerability: Selected Essays.* New York: Oxford University Press, pp. 260–88.

Watson, Gary (2011) "The Trouble with Psychopaths," in R. Wallace et al. (eds), *Reasons and Recognition: Essays on the Philosophy of T. M. Scanlon.* New York: Oxford University Press, pp. 307–31.

Widerker, David ([1995] 2003) "Libertarianism and Frankfurt's Attack of the Principle of Alternative Possibilities," in G. Watson (ed.), *Free Will.* 2nd edn, New York: Oxford University Press, pp. 177–89.

Widerker, David, and Michael McKenna (eds) (2003) *Moral Responsibility and Alternative Possibilities: Essays on the Importance of Alternative Possibilities.* Aldershot: Ashgate.

Williams, Bernard ([1976] 1981) "Moral Luck," in B. Williams, *Moral Luck: Philosophical Papers 1973–1980.* Cambridge: Cambridge University Press, pp. 20–39.

Wolf, Susan (1980) "Asymmetrical Freedom," *Journal of Philosophy* 77: 151–66.

Wolf, Susan (1987) "Sanity and the Metaphysics of Responsibility," in F. Schoeman (ed.), *Responsibility, Character, and the Emotions: New Essays on Moral Psychology.* Cambridge: Cambridge University Press, pp. 46–62.

Wolf, Susan (1990) *Freedom Within Reason.* New York: Oxford University Press.

Zimmerman, David (2003) "That Was Then, This is Now: Personal History vs. Psychological Structure in Compatibilist Theories of Autonomy," *Noûs* 37: 638–71.

Zimmerman, Michael (1986) "Negligence and Moral Responsibility," *Noûs* 20: 199–218.

Zimmerman, Michael (1988) *An Essay on Moral Responsibility.* Totowa, NJ: Rowman & Littlefield.

Zimmerman, Michael (1997) "Moral Responsibility and Ignorance," *Ethics* 107: 410–26.

Zimmerman, Michael (2008) *Living with Uncertainty.* Cambridge: Cambridge University Press.

Index